Walking the Walk

A **values-centered** approach
to building a **strong nonprofit**

Aina Gutierrez

D1597264

Interfaith Worker Justice (Attn: Communications Dept.)
1020 W. Bryn Mawr Ave.
Chicago, IL 60660
Email: info@iwj.org
Phone: 773-728-8400
www.iwj.org

Ordering Information:
Special discounts are available on quantity. For details, contact the publisher
at the address above.

Cover and Book Design: Jana Winch
Copy Editor: Betty Pessagno

ISBN 978-0-9904409-0-1

Library of Congress Control Number: 2014942011

First Printing, 2014
Printed in the United States of America

This book is dedicated to the activists and leaders who are willing to invest time and energy to learning what it takes to build successful organizations. To all of you, I say: when administrative work gets tough and boring; the tough and committed get going. Keep at it!

Acknowledgements

As a mother of three, I know that it takes a village to raise a child. As a first-time author, I learned that the same can be said about creating a book, and I am grateful for my village of support.

I'd first like to thank Interfaith Worker Justice for granting me a sabbatical that allowed me to write this book. IWJ continues to be a model of treating employees fairly, and I have been blessed to be a part of its team for so long. I am grateful to colleagues who picked up my work so I can focus on this project. Special thanks go to Kim Bobo for her guidance and input throughout the process. She is my cheerleader, mentor and friend.

I am also thankful to the readers who pored through the book and offered thoughtful comments, encouragement and lots and lots of editorial changes. Thanks so much to Pancho Arguelles, Janel Bailey, Jane Beckett, Jules Bernstein, Rebecca Cacayuran, Sung Yeon Choi-Morrow, Jonathan Currie, Adam DeRose, Cris Doby, Pablo Eisenberg, Mandy Fischer, Maritza Guzman, Mary Heidkamp, Tina Herpe, Cathy Junia, Jackie Kendall, Kathy Lyons, Regina McGraw, Vicki Meath, Pete Meyers, Doug Mork, Mary Ochs, Ruth Orme-Johnson, Victor Quintana, Marybeth Schroeder, Amy Smoucha, Jim Sessions, Linda Wagner, Jana Winch, and Allison Zidek. Your expertise and wisdom were so helpful.

I was lucky to interview more than a dozen executive directors of small nonprofits to learn about their back office issues. I certainly got a treasure trove of stories – successes, challenges, mistakes, and lucky breaks. My deepest thanks to Janet Beals Orejudos, Rick Ferguson, Kathy Lyons, Kathleen McDonald, Pete Meyers, Alfredo Pena, Jeanie Ramsey, Dino Robinson, Ileana Salinas, Marybeth Schroeder, Amber Stone, and Susan Trieschmann for your candor, openness and experience. The IWJ affiliate network of more than 40 nonprofits across the country has also taught me so much.

My family hugs and supports me everyday. Thanks Mom for your help wrangling kids and cooking dinner. Thanks to Eva, Asher and Elsa for being such good kids and for making me take breaks to have fun and think more clearly. And my love to Doug, thank you for supporting me no matter what.

Finally, I am grateful to the Ms. Foundation for funding this project and for steadfastly carrying out its mission to encourage women to be the most impactful change makers they can be. I hope I have done that.

Table of Contents

Foreword by Kim Bobo ix

Preface xi

Section 1: **Staff** 1

    Introduction – Fairness, Clarity, Generosity 1

    1. Personnel Policies 2

    2. Salaries 9

    3. Paid and Unpaid Benefits 14

    4. Best Practices on Personnel Policies. 28

    5. Legal Matters 35

    6. Evaluation 38

Section 2: **Board** 43

    Introduction – Leadership, Teamwork, Commitment 43

    1. Roles and Responsibilities of the Board 45

    2. Board versus Staff Roles 54

    3. Expectations of Board Members 58

    4. Role of the Executive Director to Help the Board Function . . . 60

    5. Composition and Structure 62

    6. Meetings 66

    7. Strengthening Your Board 69

Section 3: **Office Systems and Management** 73

    Introduction – Order, Efficiency, Practicality 73

    1. Databases 74

    2. Insurance 81

    3. Office Supplies and Furniture 84

    4. File Management. 87

    5. Getting Special Help from Experts 92

    6. Interns and Volunteers 96

        List of Long-term Volunteer Programs 98

    7. Other Organizational Policies 102

Section 4: **Compliance with Government Requirements** 104

    Introduction – Ethics, Organization, Accountability 105

    1. Government Registrations. 106

    2. Legal Requirements for Staff. .110

    3. Audits 117

    4. Tax Form 990 119

Section 5: **Finance** 122

    Introduction – Transparency, Frugality, Responsibility 122

    1. Budget 123

    2. Cash Flow 128

        Sample Cash Flow Worksheet 129

    3. Financial Management and Reporting 132

        Sample Income/Expense Report 135

    4. Internal Financial Controls 141

Section 6: **Fund Development** 143

    Introduction – Honesty, Trustworthiness, Appreciation 143

    1. Creating a Fundraising Plan 144

    2. Identifying and Building Relationships with Diverse Funding Sources . .148

    3. Thanking Your Donors 158

    4. Staying on Track 162

    5. Fundraising Resources for Small Nonprofits 165

Foreword

Anyone who has built a nonprofit knows it is hard work. Most of us got into nonprofit work because we care about the mission – we want to help people or create social change. Few of us feel great passion about filing 990's or figuring out insurance plans.

We want to build effective and powerful organizations that reflect our values, because strong organizations move the mission. To build effective and powerful organizations, we must pay attention to creating strong internal systems that support and enhance our mission. We must invest in our staff and board and the systems to support them.

For more than ten years, Aina Gutierrez helped Interfaith Worker Justice build its internal systems and consulted with dozens of affiliate organizations as they struggled to create strong organizations. The issues addressed in this handbook are common problem areas for small (and sometimes large) nonprofits. Although there are tomes about each topic in the book, there is no other handbook that explains the issues simply and clearly – and in one place.

This handbook is an invaluable resource for directors and board members of nonprofit organizations. It is written in a practical and clear style, recognizing that some issues have to be tackled incrementally. Only someone who has worked "in the trenches," like Aina, could have written such a useful handbook.

Thank you Aina for your dedication and service to the movement.

Kim Bobo
Executive Director
Interfaith Worker Justice
June 2014

Preface

If you're going to talk the talk, you've got to walk the walk.

Nonprofit leaders are a dynamic bunch. Staff, board members, and volunteers spend countless hours trying to make positive changes in the world; to grow and develop a society that is just and fair; a world that works together and is full of dignity.

These values and mission-driven beliefs are what motivate people to get up in the morning and get to work. But what if those values aren't reflected in their nonprofit workplaces? Should nonprofit directors work 50 hours a week and get paid for 30? Should nonprofits keep part-time employees so that the organization doesn't have to pay health care or retirement benefits?

Of course not. While hard decisions have to be made on shoestring budgets, nonprofit leaders need to make these decisions based on the organization's values, and not on things like what the funder wants or what the organization has historically done. This handbook was created to provide guidance on how nonprofits can operate using a values-driven approach. These common values include fairness, transparency, honesty, generosity, order, efficiency, responsibility, and equity.

This resource is for small nonprofits that have fewer than 10 employees.

A 2011 estimate from the Department of

Health and Human Services stated that about half of the country's 498,429 nonprofit employers had fewer than 10 employees[1]. That's about 200,000 organizations out there without much help on administration, operations, and personnel.

There is also so little information that is quick, practical, and helpful to those who work multiple roles and don't have time or energy to read through complicated and long, specialized documents. This handbook shares what works, based on the experiences of the author, the affiliate network of more than 40 organizations of Interfaith Worker Justice, as well as a dozen interviews with other nonprofit directors running social service agencies, small museums, arts groups, and advocacy organizations.

Interfaith Worker Justice is a national 501(c)(3) organization that engages diverse communities of faith on issues that support and help workers and their families. The organization provides training and technical assistance on capacity building issues to its affiliate network of more than 40 local organizations across the country. This handbook draws on the experiences of working with the affiliate network of interfaith committees and worker centers, but also easily applies to any small nonprofit organizations seeking change in the world.

So many of these organizations have dedicated and committed staff and boards with-

---

1. *http://meps.ahrq.gov/mepsweb/data_stats/summ_tables/insr/national/series_1/2011/tia1.htm*

out formal experience or training. They are driven by their passion and energy for the work, and their values, and not by their love of nonprofit fund accounting and fundraising. They "talk the talk."

This handbook encourages them to model strong organizational policies and practices that reflect their values and "walk the walk." This means operating internally according to values that the organizations often reflect in their program work. Staff that is not treated well doesn't feel valued. There is huge value in making enough money to support a family and offering benefits that allow hard-working people to retire with dignity. Employees feel valued in having personnel policies that are generous and transparent and that treat everyone equally.

There are other reasons why nonprofit organizations need strong administrative systems. Many organizations have opponents who don't like what the leaders are saying or doing. Weak systems make groups vulnerable. Nonprofit leaders are limited in how well they do their work when tasks that should be easy become hard. If you don't have a database, it's really hard to do a mailing. If you don't thank your donors, it's hard to keep money coming in to support the work.

A number of organizational issues, such as leadership development, coalition building, or program strategy, are not covered in this manual. Rather, the focus is on the topics that all small nonprofit organizations have less variation and yet are core to the organization's ability to do good work.

This handbook provides nonprofit staff and board members with a framework and tools to run their nonprofit organization with a values-based approach. It is a training resource and guide to help with management, finances, and operations. It will encourage staff and board members to articulate and embody its organizational values and ensure that the internal practices match those values. It is a process of solidifying an organization's culture and living within that culture.

The ideas and resources here are quick and known to work. There is no reason to reinvent the wheel when there are models out there to be borrowed and shared. The chapters are designed to stand alone for easy reference for whatever is needed. After all, leaders didn't get into this work to have organized files. But having organized files and strong systems means that staff time is used efficiently and that everyone can get back to the work that needs to be done.

Section 1

Staff

Introduction

1. Personnel Policies

2. Salaries

3. Paid and Unpaid Benefits

4. Best Practices on Personnel Policies

5. Legal Matters

6. Evaluation

Introduction – Fairness, Clarity, Generosity

In order to build a powerful organization, you almost always need staff to keep the work moving forward. If you hire staff, you need employment policies and procedures, and they must be written down and followed.

For most nonprofit organizations, staff members are their most valuable assets and the largest share of budgets go toward staff. Thus it is critical that organizations establish clear policies, ensure compliance with labor laws, and establish strong personnel practices that help staff do their best.

Human resources – all the stuff around your organization's employees and how they are treated – is one of the big challenges in running a nonprofit organization. Small nonprofits cannot afford an HR manager and so Executive Directors end up handling most personnel matters.

Because human beings are unique and sometimes unpredictable, it is important to prepare for all personnel matters and seek to develop fair, clear, and generous policies that reflect the values and culture of your organization.

Chapter 1: Personnel Policies

The moment you decide to hire a staff person is when the organization needs personnel policies. These policies clarify organizational expectations, rules, benefits, and procedures of the employee. The Board of Directors must develop these basic policies before the first staff is "on board."

In this section, staff is identified as an employee, not an independent contractor. Review the governance section of this handbook to understand employee classification and why it is important for small nonprofits to classify workers correctly.

The policy does not have to be perfect, but it does need to be in place. A personnel policy is a living document that will and should be updated as the organization grows. The easiest way to do this is to modify someone else's policy.

If you happen to be hired and there are no personnel policies in place, work with the board leadership to create policies as soon as possible.

> ### The key basic components of a personnel policy are:
> - Salaries
> - Benefits
> - Policies that promote the organization's values
> - Operations policies
> - Other employee-related policies (discipline, evaluation, grievance)

Additional policies can be developed depending on the type of work your organization does and what kind of staff needs to do the job.

Salaries and benefits are significant, and so they are addressed in separate chapters. Below are the other types of policies to consider including in your organization's personnel policies.

Policies that Promote Values

The policies below promote a particular set of values about how employees are treated and the expectations of employees that work for your organization. A few policies are also considered good governance for nonprofits and are asked about and strongly recommended in the IRS Form 990.[1]

Nondiscrimination

This policy provides equal opportunity to all hiring and promotion of staff without consideration of such things as age, gender, race, marital status, or sexual orientation. You can include whatever your board is comfortable with approving in the workplace and within the law as enforced by the Equal Employment Opportunity Commission (EEOC).

Community-based organizations might also add emphasis to hire people who come from the communities that the organization serves.

Sexual Harassment

This policy sets forth a no-tolerance environment in the workplace for sexual harassment. It should mention that the employee should make a claim if he or she has a complaint in this area.

---

1. The 990 Form inquires whether nonprofits have a whistleblower policy, conflict-of-interest policy, document retention policy, board's review of the Executive Director compensation policy, and gift acceptance policy. The IRS does not require these policies, but it is considered good governance to have those needed in place. This topic is discussed further in Section 3, Chapter 7 on Other Organizational Policies later in this book.

Whistleblower[2]

This policy is designed to encourage staff to report any illegal activity they witness within the organization. The policy should outline how someone makes a complaint, how the complaint will be investigated, and that no person will be subject to retaliation for making a complaint.

Drug-Free Workplace

This policy outlines that no one can use or possess drugs at the office or anytime during work hours. It should also explain what will happen if someone is caught with drugs (immediate termination or warning?). If you are in a state that allows medical marijuana use, you should contact the state Department of Public Health to ensure the policy abides by state law.

Workplace Safety

This policy outlines how the organization strives to make a safe and healthy workplace by responding to emergency situations, providing safe equipment and supplies for employees, and providing an easy way for staff to get any safety issues addressed.

Unions and Workers' Right to Organize

This policy indicates that the organization will not stand in the way if nonmanagement staff want to organize into a union. Nonprofits in many communities are organized, and while unions vary in their capacity to work with small groups, units can consist of as few as two nonmanagement staff. The employer should have a policy of neutrality in collective bargaining and make clear that if staff chooses to organize into a union, the organization will not interfere with these efforts in any way.

Your organization should also consider whether you need a policy on nepotism. While it is not illegal to hire relatives or others with a strong personal relationship, it is not a good practice. It could represent a conflict of interest and cause accountability and morale issues among the staff.

Operations

These procedures can set a standard for how your organization works and what is expected of staff. The types of policies you develop depend on the type of work you do. For example, if business travel is required at your organization, a mileage reimbursement process should be written out, abided by, and enforced by the board and Executive Director.

Hours of Work

The hours of work expected of staff is important information that should be shared with them at the beginning of employment. Workplaces are increasingly requiring varying hours, which can create confusion amongst staff. Information that should be included in this policy is minimum expectations of hours (35 or 40 hours a week for full-time staff?), lunch or other breaks, overtime and compensatory time policies and flextime policies if applicable. It may also be important to note office hours if the office has set hours when employees must be present.

Timesheets and Payroll

Timesheets are important records even if staff is salaried and/or exempt from overtime. They are helpful for purposes of keeping an eye on workload issues for staff and they also are used for recording vacation and other paid or unpaid leave. A brief sample policy is as follows:

> All employees are required to submit timesheets indicating hours worked and other information as may be required. These should be submitted at least three days prior to the end of each pay period. Timesheets are a permanent record and provide the documentation on which payroll checks and grant reimbursements are issued.

---

2. Policy from IRS Form 990.

Payroll: All employees will be paid twice a month, on the 15th and the last day of the month. If payday falls on a weekend day, the employee will be paid on the previous Friday.

Expense Reimbursement

This policy is very important as it clarifies what constitutes work-related expenses and expectations on spending the organization's resources. Many organizations offer cash advances for travel costs. But if you have an organizational credit card and staff have individual accounts, you should have a section on classifying credit card expenses and providing receipts for every expense. Your auditors will thank you!

Business Credit Card Policy

This policy includes expectations for those who hold a business credit card, and stipulates appropriate charges and reporting requirements. Be very cautious on issuing individual cards to staff members and have strong policies on making sure cards are used properly.

Honoraria

This is money paid to staff for speaking, writing, training, or other work. Any work-related activities done that receive honoraria should be given to the organization. If a staff member has a particular skill that is not related to the work of the organization, he/she should keep that honoraria as long as the work is performed on their own free time.

Employee-Related Policies

These procedures are important additions as they provide structure in situations that hopefully are rare occurrences, such as discipline, grievances, or exit procedures. Having these policies in place provides clarity when difficult situations do arise, ensuring that any personnel issue is addressed in an objective and a timely way.

Discipline and Dismissal

This part of your personnel policy should be drafted very thoughtfully and carefully. Having a fair, transparent, detailed, and clear disciplinary or grievance procedure allows for a fair and more objective approach to what can often be a difficult process.

What Not To Do

Many personnel policies regarding this issue read something like the following: "An employee may be terminated with or without following any of the other procedures above. Employment is at will."

Why we shouldn't make our employees "at-will."

Most states in the United States have at-will employment laws, which means that the employer may fire the employee at any time, with or without a reason. The employer, for example, could simply not like the color of your shirt and fire you the next day.

At-will sections in personnel policies are meant to protect the employers and give them the freedom to fire people whenever needed. Many people think this is a good practice. Proponents of at-will policies believe the practice allows businesses to stay afloat when times are lean by cutting staff quickly to save money, and minimizes lawsuits from employees.

However such laws affect productivity, morale, and community among staff who as a result feel they are treated as disposable. Staff should experience trust and support from their organizations. Organizations should treat each individual as a contributing member to the staff and try to meet individual leadership and training needs.

It is true that sometimes people need to be fired. But a good discipline and dismissal process can create avenues of letting folks go for just cause, not just because it's convenient or easy to fire someone under at-will practices. Just-cause dismissal places a value on treating employees with respect and dignity and, when things don't work out, provides a way to keep your organization strong.

The value of a good disciplinary procedure is to try to keep and support all staff within the organization. For that reason, discipline should be progressive and transparent and involve a specific process in which employees are notified about issues that need to be addressed and are given an opportunity to correct those issues.

There are generally two reasons employees are disciplined:

- **Unsatisfactory performance**. Not representing the organization in a professional manner, failure to do what the job requires, or absenteeism.

- **Misconduct**. Failing to abide by job procedures, violating personnel policies, or stealing organizational dollars or property.

Before an employee is formally disciplined, discuss the issue and address it. Everyone makes mistakes, and decline in work product or conduct happens for many different reasons. Generally, employees are hired in the first place because they have the skills and gifts needed to do the job. It's worth trying to work with someone to improve. It also can be more efficient for the organization to try and help someone already familiar with the work versus firing and hiring new people who need to be trained.

However, when attempts to address the issue don't work, disciplinary steps need to be taken. The steps are as follows: (1) Employee is issued a written need for improvement statement, (2) employee receives a written warning, (3) employee is placed under disciplinary probation, and (4) employee is dismissed. Each step includes a meeting between the employee, supervisor, and Executive Director (or two board members with the Executive Director if the discipline is for the director herself). The written and specific report should include identification of the issue, a clear timeline to resolve the issue, how it needs to be resolved, and what will happen if the issue is or is not resolved.

During a disciplinary meeting, you want to be sure to share the entire process with the employee and show where this meeting fits into the disciplinary process. No one should be surprised when fired. Actually, no one should be surprised either when disciplined. People generally know when they aren't doing good work or relating well with their peers.

In the case of criminal activity, gross misconduct, or other extreme situations, the organization should reserve the right to skip any disciplinary steps and terminate the employee immediately. If the organization is certain that criminal activity has occurred, the director should notify the police.

 Here are a few other tips when you are going through a discipline and dismissal process with an employee:

- Keep good files. When issues with employees start to arise, take notes on the occurrence and record the date when something happened so that you can refer to it later if necessary. Written discipline and dismissal documents should be kept in the employee's personnel file. The employee should also get a copy. Occasionally, instances of disgruntled employees and unemployment claims that aren't valid do come up, and it is so helpful to have personnel files to tell the story.

- Bring someone else into difficult meetings. If you are a supervisor and know a conversation will be difficult with an employee, ask the Executive Director (or appropriate board member if that is okay with the director) to join the meeting. Find someone who is a calming presence and will be helpful. If you are an employee and you are a union member, you have the right to have a union representative present in the meeting. Having a third party present can be very useful for setting an appropriate and professional tone to the interaction.

- Keep communication flowing. Despite personnel issues, work still needs to be done. Don't shut out your staff and start reassigning work if there's a discipline problem. If the intention is to work together to fix a problem, the employee needs opportunities to show his or her efforts to change. Employees are encouraged to ask their supervisors questions and to ask for more information if needed. If you want to stay in your job, you will need to continue to build relationships with your colleagues and show your ability for change.

Grievance Procedure

A grievance procedure is a complaint process related to the personnel policy and/or the supervisor's interpretation of the personnel policy. Essentially, it gives employees a more formal way to work out issues within the organization. It also usually provides an ad-

vocate to support the employee through the process. For union members, this is Weingarten Rights.

If your organization has a union contract, the union typically files grievances on behalf of one or more employees or on behalf of the union institutionally. The union has a central role in addressing grievances, so the procedure is quite detailed in the contract.

If your organization is not unionized but has a personnel policy, any individual can present a grievance.

Spelling out these procedures is critical. It ensures that everyone has the same information regarding process, timeframes, and information needed to have a thorough procedure. Many of us certainly wouldn't remember what was needed if it wasn't written down!

Resignation

The personnel policy should make clear what is expected of employees and the organization when someone leaves. An example is below:

> Employees who voluntarily resign shall give the following notice:
>
> Employed from 6 months to three years – 2 weeks
> Employed more than 3 years – 3 weeks

Evaluation

Information regarding the staff evaluation process can be found in Chapter 6 on page 38. But a brief policy should be developed that sets annual evaluation as the standard for all employees. An example is below:

> All staff will receive a formal evaluation before the end of the year. The evaluation process should encourage communication and provide opportunities for all staff to evaluate what they do well and what areas need to be strengthened. The evaluation seeks input from varied parties who work with the employee and culminates with a written report and meeting with the employee's supervisor.

Using the Policies

Policies don't have much authority if they aren't used uniformly within the organization. Each staff person should be given a copy of the personnel policies, and the policies should be reviewed as a part of the new employee's orientation. The board chair should also have a copy of the policies and be familiar with them.

Some sections of the policies will be used more than others. For example, most folks will be very familiar with the salary and benefits sections of the policy, but not remember what to do when a disciplinary need arises. It is for this reason that those who address personnel issues most often (likely the Executive Director) should always keep a copy of the policy handy.

Having clear policies is important for two reasons: First, everyone wants to be treated fairly. Organizations should acknowledge the unique qualities of each employee and strive for equity between employees. Exceptions are not a good idea because staff will believe someone is getting special treatment. Second, clear policies are easily enforced. The director or staff supervisor can remove personal feelings from the situation and simply follow the policies that the board approved for the organization. It is always important to be objective and professional.

For situations that are outside the personnel policies, be very thoughtful and cautious on setting precedent. It's impossible to create policies for every little thing, and frankly, it's not always the best use of everyone's time. However, that means that a whole set of decisions get made without a policy structure. This is okay, but leadership needs to be thoughtful about setting precedent with these types of decisions.

For example, a staff person has requested permission to work from home two days a week, and you don't have a policy on flexible time. If this request is granted, it will be assumed by other staff that they would be granted the same request since it was given to one person already. Unless you want everyone to be able to work from home two days a week, be careful in making the first step in granting the request.

Always think about the long-term effects of making these types of decisions. Document the decision and reasons in the staff member's personnel file. Also consider developing policies (like flextime as mentioned above) if an issue is raised that could provide difficulties for the organization in the future.

Changing the Policies

The personnel policies need to be reviewed and updated as the need arises. Policy revisions are made because someone is using the policies and has noticed a gap that needs to be addressed; the organization had a bad experience with someone and needs a policy so it doesn't happen again in the future; or operational changes have been made that require new or revised policies. Staff should be informed every time a policy changes.

One nonprofit organization had a challenging experience recently with its flextime practices. A growing number of staff kept asking to work from home for various writing projects. The director agreed to test a work from home on Fridays practice for all staff whose jobs did not require them to be in the office. Unfortunately, staff just stopped showing up for work on Fridays, and it didn't seem like much work was being done at all! The board asked to address this issue by providing more detailed information on when staff needed to be in the office and on the approval process of being able to work from home.

The Board of Directors sets policies for the organization, and so it needs to approve all personnel policy changes. Staff can develop and draft policies (with board help if it's useful) and should have a personnel committee or executive committee review the changes and provide feedback before going to the full board for a vote of approval.

You don't want to have policy changes be a constant agenda item for board meetings, so if the policy changes aren't urgent, it might be prudent to present a few changes at a time and get them all approved together.

Finally, any approved changes to personnel policies should be noted in the board meeting minutes as decisions made by the board. The policy itself should also reflect the date of the last revision, noted at the bottom of the document. It is helpful to know when a policy was last approved, so that periodic reviews can be scheduled.

Strong personnel policies are a core way of showing the value that employees have within the organization, presenting the values of the organization, and strengthening and protecting the organization in the long term. Both staff and board members have a responsibility to ensure that policies are clear, detailed, and up to date.

Chapter 2: Salaries

The amount your organization decides to pay your employees depends on a number of factors such as location, cost of living, market for similar job positions in your community, and responsibility within the organization.

However, as much as is possible, advocate for generous salaries. Some nonprofit organizations keep salaries low to identify or relate more with their constituencies. Most say they can't afford to pay more. And yet, low salaries hurt organizations.

Nonprofits need to be able to recruit and keep talent on the staff. Many young workers have school loans and other debt. They have families and make enough money to support those families. They might want to buy a house someday and go on a vacation or two! Passion about a cause should not require a staff member to ensure economic hardship.

There are also race and gender dynamics at play in nonprofit compensation. The wage gap between men and women, as well as between races and ethnic communities, continues to be a problem, and it affects those willing to work in the nonprofit field. Low pay decreases the diversity of leadership on economic, gender and racial levels.

Organizations need to keep talented staff.

> *"I had a long-time part-time employee leave because she needed higher pay to help her kids afford college. I didn't have the budget to increase her hours."*

> *"One of my best employees asked for a significant salary increase and better benefits. I wish I could have given her what she needed, but couldn't afford it. After two months, she left for a better-paying job."*

It is so hard to have continuity and build and expand work without consistent staff. It is also heartbreaking to not be able to support those who do good work and want to stay, but need to leave to support their family obligations.

Morale also tends to be low when there's low pay. If staff doesn't make much, it also generally means there aren't many resources to actually do the work. Also, when employees are struggling to make ends meet it can create stress that impacts the individual and his or her work.

Pay fairly and generously. Consider the following when setting employee compensation:

Pay Fairly

Research comparable positions of other organizations in your area to see what others are offering. What is the salary range for similar positions in other communities[3]? Also, what is the private-sector comparison for employees with similar skills? At a minimum, offer a salary that is competitive with that of other folks. Management staff or board members should consider creating long-term plans with a strategy to increase salaries over time to make them closer to the private sector and should stick to making that a financial priority.

Promote pay equity as a value within your organization. Many suggest that a good ratio between highest paid and lowest paid staff should be anywhere from 3:1 to 5:1. There should also not a wide gap between the highest salary and second highest salary. One large nonprofit in Chicago that recently closed had a lot of disgruntled employees and very low morale around wages (among other issues). The organization, which served low-income people, was paying the lowest

---

3. Check out Roadmap Consulting's 2012 compensation survey, *The Wages of Peace and Justice.*

paid staff about $20,000/year for full-time work, and the CEO was making more than $300,000/year. When budget cuts came, staff members were angry about salary freezes; one source of this anger was the wage gap and the failure of those at the top to share the burden of those cuts.

Be careful to promote equity not only between top and bottom, but also between those who have similar responsibility and accountability. Folks don't need the same position or job title to be equitable. They may be carrying similar weight and leadership within the organization.

Another good principle is to pay staff for actual hours worked.

> *"I'm paid for 35 hours a week but generally work 50-60 hours."*

> *"I'm part-time, which is about 15 hours a week. But the board knows I have to work much more than that."*

Organizations should establish a culture in which employees are paid for all the work they do and all the hours they put in.

Depending on the position, this could result in legal issues if the employee is nonexempt and should be paid for overtime. For salaried exempt employees, the person isn't paid hourly and doesn't qualify for overtime. But an organization shouldn't have a culture in which employees are expected to consistently work much more than what they are paid for.

When organizations do not fully compensate employees for their time, everyone loses. Employees burn out and don't feel valued. Poor treatment of employees is not a sustainable budgeting model. If the staff person who is paid for 15 hours a week leaves, it will be incredibly difficult to find someone to replace that person and be willing to work 30 hours for such low pay.

Pay Generously

All employees should make AT LEAST a living wage. Check out this Universal Wage Formula to see how much that would be in your community, *www.universallivingwage. org.* A living wage is still very modest, but much more realistic than a minimum wage rate.

If an employee is nonexempt (see Section 4 on governance to learn more) as defined by the Fair Labor Standards Act (FLSA), the organization must pay overtime for more than 40 hours worked in a workweek. Because this gets costly quickly, your personnel policy should require approval of overtime before it happens.

Do not promise future increases as a part of salary and setting compensation. Fundraising requires a certain amount of optimism. It requires not only belief in the mission, but also that strategies will work and the budget will be met or exceeded. But many things are outside of your control, and sometimes there isn't the money that you had hoped for. So when hiring, be honest with staff about the salary and don't promise things that might not be delivered. Promise only what is being offered and anything else that can be concretely given.

Setting Salaries

To foster a culture of transparency, objectivity, and equity, it is best to have a salary schedule that provides salary ranges for each staff person within the organization. It should be discussed with each employee when hired so that they understand the overall picture of salaries and how each person's salary impacts the budget.

The schedule should be drafted by the Executive Director (with help from appropriate board members or staff if helpful to the director) and reviewed by the Board as a part of its work to create and approve a budget. The Executive Director has the authority to make an exception to the schedule, but it should be done in conjunction with the board and should stay within the approved budget.

The Executive Director's salary is set and approved by the Board of Directors. It is also adjusted by the board as necessary.

Adjusting Salaries

Any change in salary, for good or bad, is heavily dependent on meeting the budget. Organizations implement salary increases in many different ways, but should be careful to make sure salary changes reflect the values and culture of the organization. Maintaining open communication, seeking input from the staff, being transparent with the board and ownership of the budget, and showing a budget commitment to generous salaries will make the process as positive and thoughtful as possible. Here are a few budget scenarios and salary adjustment suggestions:

A tight, but decent budget year.
The budget was met but just barely. There's not much extra wiggle room for the next year. In this context, you might provide a combination of the following:

- *Cost of Living Annual Increases (COLA).*[4] These increases keep the value of salaries in line with inflation. The federal government provides a percentage COLA increase that you can try to meet for your staff.

- *Year-end bonuses.* If you aren't confident enough in next year's budget to increase the salary base, a per-person bonus might be an option. This is usually a flat rate for

each employee of $250–$1,500, depending on how much money is available.

A successful year.
Yes! The budget is met and there is some money for salary increases. This, of course, is the best scenario and most uplifting for staff. A few types of increases you might consider include:

- *Step increases.* This is more money for more work. With the value of compensating those fairly for the amount of work, responsibility, and accountability within the organization, some staff might have taken on additional work that should be reflected in their pay. This does not have to be done for everyone, so this compensation should be considered in this context in addition to a COLA increase or bonus for all staff.

- *Base pay increases.* This is simply increasing the salary of an employee. For Executive Directors, it would be hard to take on more work than the job requires, since most directors do so much already. The director (for other staff) and board (for Executive Director) can increase base pay as is possible. Just be careful that the pay is adjusted at a level that can be sustained in the future.

Some organizations also provide merit increases based on work product and performance, although merit systems tend to be controversial with small nonprofits. Many believe that merit-based increases create a competitive environment that is counter to the teamwork that is needed in a small organization, and gives too much subjective authority to the people setting the increases.

A financial crisis.
A significant deficit means that serious cuts need to be made. Hopefully, if there is a crisis

---

4. *www.ssa.gov/OACT/COLA/latestCOLA.html*

brewing, staff is informed about it early on and everything is done to try and raise more money and cut expenses before getting to salaries.

Before layoffs are put on the table, the organization might consider some of the following ideas to save money on payroll:

- Not rehiring for a position that is open or where someone has left voluntarily.

- Salary freezes and no salary increases.

- Salary cuts. One organization's staff decided that a 20 percent pay cut for everyone was better than a layoff.

- Furlough days. These are similar to salary cuts but give staff unpaid time off. Some might value the time off with families or even pick up extra work elsewhere.

If layoffs are inevitable, go through the following steps to make the most objective decision and determine what is best for the organization:

- Follow the personnel policy procedure or collective bargaining agreement related to layoffs. It is in these difficult situations that procedures become important, not only to have a process to follow but to know that the process is objective and fair. If you don't have procedures, it's a good idea to develop them when things are stable.

- Consider the organization's annual goals. What positions are absolutely necessary to complete the work and vision set forth by the board?

- Review any restricted funding requests. Are there positions specifically funded by grants or corporations that can't be adjusted? If the work committed to isn't completed, could that jeopardize future funding and lead to additional budget problems in the future?

- Evaluate how work can continue to be done with layoffs. Can current staff pick up additional work? Can this work be put off, or a program discontinued? It will be very important to make sure current staff are not overburdened with extra work; otherwise they will look for other jobs.

- Examine the current budget and budgets for the next couple of years. Will layoffs provide enough stability, not only this year but in the next couple of years? If possible, plan ahead so that no one has to experience this demoralizing situation again the next year.

- Be sure to put all decisions made related to layoffs in writing. Talk about the economic factors that led to the layoffs, the considerations made, and the decisions that were made as a result of those considerations. All layoffs should be objective, fair, and in the best interest of the organization. Having a written record is crucial not only for organizational history but also in the event that any issue arises with a former staff person later on.

Paying Executive Directors

Most Executive Directors are overworked, and many, especially those running small social justice organizations, are underpaid. They don't sleep at night worrying about having enough money for payroll, and they spend their time doing everything from meeting with major donors to unclogging a toilet.

A few things directors have done in order to keep things afloat that are ill advised:

- Lent the organization $40,000 of personal funds to make the budget

- Voluntarily took a 40 percent pay cut for six months

- Refused to take a pay raise because it

meant having to raise more money

- Worked 60 hours a week while being paid for 30 hours a week

All of these actions are well-intentioned to help with short-term crises, but overall they are harmful to the organization. These actions are not financially sustainable, and in addition they provide precedent and expectations for these types of sacrifices in the future, which isn't fair to future leadership. For example, the director who lent the organization personal funds ended up being asked to leave by the board, which meant the board had to quickly come up with the money to pay the person back before leaving the organization. How awkward and terrible!

Board members should provide support and counsel to the director regarding salary. Board members decide the Executive Director's salary and should be sure it is documented in board minutes every year, even if no change is made in compensation. If the board members increase salary, they should be prepared to raise the additional funds to cover it. Don't allow individuals to loan money to the organization. Don't support budgeting practices that are not sustainable. And be sure that your director is paid fairly for his/her time.

TIP *Other back-office tips on wages:*

- Keep complete files of employee salaries, including adjustments. See Chapter 4 – *Best Practices for Personnel Policies* on page 28 for guidance on preparing personnel files. Paperwork should reflect any and all salary increases.

- Designate one staff person to handle all human resource matters, including salary policies and procedures. Doing so ensures consistency and accountability in implementing salary policies and other organizational policies developed by the board. In small nonprofits, the Executive Director often takes on this role.

- Educate and involve staff in the budgeting process. This helps them understand how salary decisions are made and what impact that has in other areas of the organization. That burden should not just fall to the Executive Director and the board.

Of course, there are other ways to value employees, not just through salaries. Providing strong benefits, flexible work schedules, comfortable hours, dignity and voice in decision making in the organization all matter. Executive Directors and board members tout these benefits as reasons employees want to work for their organization. But nonprofit staff turnover can be high, and it's because very practically speaking, everyone has to meet his/her basic needs and provide for family. Generous benefits are seldom enough to keep good staff if they can't meet their economic needs.

Chapter 3: Paid and Unpaid Benefits

Although budgetary constraints can make it difficult to provide health care, retirement benefits, or wages that compete with the private sector, the nonprofit sector can (and should) be a leader in providing generous paid time off and flexible time work arrangements for employees. Employees value generous paid time off and flextime policies. These nonmonetary benefits are a strong way to show employees that they are valued and raise the bar for all workers to have fair and generous benefits.

Instead of adding benefits piecemeal or designing benefits around particular individuals, help the board decide what values and priorities the organization wants to reflect in its employees' benefit packages. Health care and retirement benefits are expensive, so it may not be possible to provide everyone with what they want and need.

The mission of the nonprofit often has a distinct impact on what benefits are offered. Health-related groups often provide the full cost of health insurance, or a women's rights group might have generous parental leave policies. These mission-related values should also be discussed.

One way to work toward building a strong benefits package is to set financial priorities over time that will build up benefits to desired levels. Although nonprofit boards may not be able to provide everything they want to staff, they should be clear about what they can currently provide and set priorities for benefits that could be added in the future.

Paid Benefits

Health Care

Providing good-quality health care for staff is extremely expensive and is often the most costly piece of a benefits package. However, employers have a responsibility to give all their workers access to health care – and nonprofit employees are no exception.

Nonprofit employers can provide health coverage to staff. Options range from offering monetary support for health-care-related expenses to full coverage. Find a starting point for your organization and work with your leadership to make health care coverage an organizational budget priority.

Nonprofit managers are hopeful that the Affordable Care Act will help small businesses and nonprofits offer affordable health care options for employees.

The three key aspects of this important legislation are as follows:

- Nonprofits with less than 50 employees will not pay a penalty for not offering health insurance.

- Small nonprofits that offer health care may qualify for a payroll tax credit. The amount of the credit varies depending on the number of employees and salaries for those employees. To claim the credit, there's an additional form that you, your auditor, or your accountant need to complete with your organization's 990 form.[5]

- Small nonprofits with fewer than 50 employees have access to the health care exchanges for their employees. This will hopefully bring more affordable premiums, although no one yet knows how affordable these plans will be. The type of exchange for your group is based on the

---

5. *www.irs.gov/uac/Small-Business-Health-Care-Tax-Credit-for-Small-Employers*

state in which you live. An easy survey and checklist to share options can be found at *www.healthcare.gov*. Also, a health care broker can help provide the best options for your organization and staff.

The intention behind the Affordable Care Act is to get more people insured. This is a very good thing and one that small organizations should take advantage of right away.

The suggestions below are guidelines based on what is known at this moment and may need modification to reflect future public policies and tax laws.[6]

> Whatever choice your organization makes, be sure to think about the long-term benefits and costs to your organization. If your organization plans to add employees in the future, it may be worth choosing a health care plan that has the capacity to accommodate a larger number of employees down the road.

★☆☆☆ **Level 1 – Provide reimbursement for health care-related expenses.**

This first level provides reimbursement if an employee has his/her own plan, is covered under a spouse's health care plan, or is not insured at all. Reimbursement can also be given to full-time or part-time employees on a prorated basis.

Offer reimbursement as much as possible. For example, $3,000 for a full-time employee isn't much and wouldn't cover any individual's annual costs, but it is a significant help. You could also consider providing the equivalent of whatever the monthly premium is for your organization's plan (or research what the rough cost of a plan would be) and then reimburse that amount to each employee.

This is a bare bones option for an organization that is currently not offering any coverage. Keep in mind that any reimbursement may be taxable income, so be sure to check current tax laws before moving forward.

★★☆☆ **Level 2 – Find health care plans for your employees without offering it yourself. And have the organization pay as much as possible for those plans.**

This level works when each eligible full-time employee finds affordable health care coverage for up to a set amount a year. Part-time employees, usually those working 20 hours or more a week, could receive partial coverage. It would be very dependent on who is on your staff at any moment, but there are often options for staff to join someone else's health care plan or get their own. A few ideas include the following:

- Find a larger umbrella organization through which you can get employee health insurance. If you have a fiscal sponsor, that organization might be able to add you to its health care plan. Unions also sometimes offer health care plans to their members.

- Explore having employees join their spouse/partners' health care plan.

- Pay COBRA insurance from the employee's last job. Your organization could pay the COBRA costs for the employee to be covered under the group rate from their last employer. This is only a temporary solution, as employees are usually covered only 12–18 months after they have left their job. And COBRA is often quite expensive.

- Reimburse employees for individual health care plans. Depending on the employee, this option might be more affordable than any other.

---

6. *www.healthcare.gov*

Please keep in mind that any of the options above may be considered taxable income for each employee, so check current tax requirements.

★★★☆ **Level 3 – Offer a group health care plan for individual employees who qualify and health care reimbursement for those who don't qualify or are on other plans.**

Most insurance companies will cover employees who are considered full-time, or work at least 30 hours a week. Some will cover employees who work at least 20 hours a week. You need at least two employees to get a group plan. If you have just one employee, that person could get an individual plan that is paid for directly by the organization.

In order to qualify for the Health Care Tax Credit for small employers (see above), employers must pay at least 50 percent of the monthly premiums.

Individual Coverage. In most small, social justice groups, the organization pays for as much of the individual's coverage as possible. The organization must pay at least 50 percent of the premium in order to qualify for the government's Health Care Tax Credit.

Family/Dependent Coverage. This varies greatly among organizations, but in general there is an effort to offer family coverage and pay for some part of it. Unfortunately, the range on this benefit varies widely, notably:

- No coverage for family or dependents

- $100/month toward family coverage if using the organization's health care plan

- 33 to 75 percent coverage by the organization

- A spousal surcharge. This is an increasingly common practice: $50 per month or more is provided if an employee's spouse is eligible for coverage through his or her

employer and the spouse elects not to take that coverage. In this case, the organization covers the full premium. This option is popular with spouses and partners who are college or graduate students, where health care is offered but generally is not very good.

★★★★ **Level 4 – Health care coverage at no cost to the employee.**

Providing full individual or family health care coverage at no cost to the employee is an enormous benefit to provide. It is an increasingly rare occurrence in the nonprofit or for-profit world. However, providing this benefit is such an affirmation of care and support to employees and their families that many organizations have decided to make it a budget priority, even allowing it to take precedence over other benefits such as higher wages and retirement.

How to get a health care plan if you don't have one.

1. Find an insurance broker.
An insurance broker is a valuable resource in helping one to understand the complicated health care world. The cost of a broker is folded into the quotes from health care companies, and the commission varies depending on your state. The cost should always be the same, regardless of which broker you choose, and it is well worth it.

A broker is someone with whom you should build a good relationship and can help your organization with the following:

- Quotes for health care plans from multiple companies

- Education on types of health care plans, calculation of costs, and updates on implementation of the Affordable Care Act and public health care plans

- Annual updates on the plan, new quotes,

and ideas to help keep plans that are affordable

- Education of staff on how the plans work and other benefits-related questions

- Enrollment and coverage information on the benefits offered by your organization

- COBRA distribution to employees when they leave

- Support when problems arise, such as denied coverage or confusing paperwork

- Wellness programs and newsletters on how to stay in good health

A good broker serves as a resource for help with benefits, so it is very important to find the right broker for your organization.

When looking for a broker, be sure to interview more than one person for the job. While brokers are generally paid the same amount, not all brokers are the same nor do they provide the same services. Find a few names of folks who have experience working with small nonprofits and are recommended by people you know and trust to make good decisions. Be sure to think about:

- Experience and knowledge with insurance products. Make sure the person is fully knowledgeable about companies and plans in your area, the national health care reform landscape, and where to go for assistance if he or she doesn't know the answer to your questions. Many brokers work in groups and help each other, so you should understand what kind of access you have to outside resources.

- Compatibility. This may seem trivial, but if you don't like the person, don't hire him/her. Your broker should be someone you're comfortable asking for help and advice. If you don't like the person, you won't use that person.

- References. Ask for references from folks in organizations similar to yours, and then call them. It's a great way to get the inside scoop on the broker and the pros and cons of working with the broker's firm.

Also find out what other services or wellness programs your broker offers. One nonprofit had a broker for many years who encouraged employees to try and fix their own benefits problems and didn't provide the office with any kind of wellness education or programming (such as flu shots). Staff didn't realize that such things could be offered until they met with a new firm and discovered a number of expanded services offered for the same money. The new firm offered not only newsletters and flu shots but access to an attorney if legal issues came up, direct communication with broker when employees had problems, and COBRA administration when employees left. Ask about other services offered and compare notes between brokers.

After you interview a few brokers, pick one. Don't ask two brokers to get health care quotes for you. All brokers get the same rates from health care companies. Insurance companies don't like to waste their time providing multiple quotes for the same organization and could very well decide not to cover your employees.

2. Talk to those who will be covered.
At the beginning of the process, involve those who will be most impacted: the employees who will be covered by the plan. Have one-on-one confidential conversations on the health care needs and wants of your employees, stressing that they might not get everything they want with regard to health care. This information will be very helpful to you in selecting the best plan and coverage. For example, high deductible plans are very popular right now as plans that can save the

employer money, but if the deductible is too high the employee might not be able to pay it him/herself. Or if the employee has regular or expensive health care needs, it may not be a less expensive option.

Also be sure you understand plan options for full- and part-time employees. There are often limitations to coverage for those who work less than 30 hours a week.

3. Get quotes.

Your broker should learn about your organization's employees (name, date of birth, zip code) and develop a spreadsheet that outlines a variety of plans and costs based on those who need to be covered. When choosing a plan you should review the types of plans carefully and consider the overall cost to the employee. For example, high deductible plans have a much lower monthly premium but can cost the employee a large amount of money if the organization doesn't cover some of the deductible. Or your organization might be okay with a smaller network and lower cost if staff uses similar and covered health care providers.

4. Review the final options with the organization's director and/or board.

It is never wise to make a big organizational decision alone. Review the options with key staff and/or the board personnel committee or someone knowledgeable on the board and make sure it's a good plan.

5. Talk to those who will be covered (again).

Have the broker come in and talk through the options and answer any questions about the health care plan, the invoicing process, and keeping good records. Give the broker an opportunity to build relationships with other staff.

When does the health care plan go into effect?
Most insurance companies allow employees

to join plans on the first of the month following their start date. You may want to keep this in mind when establishing start dates for new employees, to make sure that they don't have any gap in coverage from a previous job.

TIP *Other tips on buying and maintaining health care plans*

- Bundle products to save money. A lot of insurance companies offer different types of insurance and are willing to offer a discount if you buy more than one product at a time. This can save quite a bit of money, so ask for quotes from each company for everything that is applicable, such as health care, dental, vision, or disability insurance.

- Review your insurance cost every year before renewal and prepare to get new quotes if needed. Some years the cost of insurance goes up just a bit, and other years renewal cost can increase more than 15 percent! This price spike can really impact the budget, so ask your broker to get new quotes and start the buying process again if needed. Employees are usually open to changing if it means saving the organization money, although you should try to minimize the requirement to change doctors. Beware that some insurance companies offer a lower rate to get you to change companies and then increase the rates drastically in subsequent years. Your broker should be able to help you make a choice that offers cost savings and fair pricing for multiple years.

- Explore cost-sharing options with other employers. Sometimes employers can work together to find an affordable health care option by sharing the cost of a family plan or one organization reimbursing the other for health care-related costs. For example, if both organizations offer an employee and her spouse health care and a family plan costs $15,000, the organizations can agree to split the cost so that the family is on one employer's plan and the other employer pays $7,500 annually.

Retirement

Offering retirement benefits aids in recruiting and keeping talented staff by providing much needed long-term savings to employees. It also reflects the organization's commitment to providing its valuable staff with long-term benefits.

As with health care benefits, organizations should make retirement savings a long-term organizational budget priority and work toward offering this benefit, even if it can't be done immediately. Below are suggestions on how to get started:

★☆☆ Level 1 – Offer payroll deductions to employees' IRA accounts with no employer contribution.

This would be a bare bones first step in adding something about retirement in your personnel policy and in building toward providing a stronger benefit in the future.

This option is easy to set up and doesn't require any reporting by the employer. It also gives the employee an easy way to contribute to a retirement account, which makes it more likely he or she will do so. For more information on this option, click on *www.irs. gov/Retirement-Plans/Establishing-a-Payroll-Deduction-IRA.*

The biggest downside of this option is that the employer is not making any financial con-

tribution to the employees; retirement funds. It is also the employees' responsibility to open the IRA account and provide the right paperwork to set up the deductions.

★★☆ Level 2 – Offer Simplified Employee Pension (SEP) account or Savings Incentive Match Plan for Employees (Simple) IRA account with an employer contribution.

According to the IRS, these two types of retirement accounts are the easiest ways for small nonprofits to provide a benefit to its employees.[7] The biggest difference between them is that SEP does not require a minimum employer contribution, so the employee wouldn't risk having to close the account if he or she weren't able to make a minimum contribution owing to a bad financial year. The Simple IRA, as of this writing, requires an employer to provide a matching contribution of up to 3 percent of compensation, or 2 percent for each eligible employee. Application information and setup can be found on the IRS website.

These accounts provide modest reporting requirements for the employer, but the burden is still on the employees to set up and open their own IRA accounts. This can be challenging, especially for those employees who are not comfortable with financial matters. It also puts a burden on the organization's leadership to make sure employees have set up and opened their accounts and are receiving the benefit.

★★★ Level 3 – Offer a defined contribution retirement plan – 401(k) or 403(b).

A defined contribution plan, like a 401(k) or 403(b), is a way for employers to offer employees a more traditional retirement benefit.

---

7. *www.irs.gov/Retirement-Plans/Plan-Sponsor/Types-of-Retirement-Plans-1*

This benefit requires quite a bit more work for the employer to set up and administer. Here are two ideas:

1. *Join an umbrella plan with other organizations.*

Some United Ways, community foundations, and nonprofit associations offer umbrella plans that are looking for nonprofit members, so it's worth asking around to see there's a plan in your area that your organization could join.

The major benefit of joining an umbrella plan is that your organization is not itself liable or responsible for dealing with all the record keeping, reporting, and managing of the plan. This is a significant benefit that can save time and money. Just be sure to explore the following when looking at other plans:

- *Fees.* What are the fees? Usually there are annual fees, per-person fees, and fees depending on the funds in the portfolio. All that should be easily identified and spelled out.

- *Types of funds offered.* Are a variety of funds being offered? Are there socially responsible options? Who manages those funds? Do the funds offer competitive returns? What kind of flexibility is offered to participants? Are the plans/funds packaged, or do employees choose their own portfolio?

- *Plan Administration.* Who is responsible for record keeping, IRS reporting, and Employee Retirement Income Security Act (ERISA) compliance?

- *User services.* Is it easy for employees to get plan information and access their records? Employees should have easy online access. Ask for a demonstration (demo) if plan information is not clear. How often can employees change funds? Do they have

direct access to a financial advisor with questions? Can someone come to the office once a year to connect with folks and provide updated advice?

- *Communication.* Who do employees contact with questions? What other types of reports will the organization and its employees receive?

- *Other requirements.* Some plans require employer contributions or membership into their organization. Be sure to include those costs and work into your assessment of joining a new plan.

2. *Set up and administer your own retirement plan.*

The most comprehensive way to offer retirement is to set up your own plan.

There are three important pieces to develop a retirement plan:

- *Financial Advisor/Broker.* This person helps manage the plan, enrolls employees, explains the plan, helps employees figure out their risk tolerance, and helps set up the funds in the plan. Look for someone whom you like, has experience with nonprofit organizations, is easy to reach, and is willing to be contacted directly by employees and come in once a year to talk with them. Also, this person should be someone whose fees aren't too high.

- Independent brokers are desirable because they don't work for one company and can offer more options. Commission brokers make a percentage based on the sales of products, which means there is an incentive to sell, sell, sell. This can lead to getting advice that is not the best and most objective.

- *Money Manager.* The money manager offers the funds or fund packages to your group and manages the plan's assets. Look for someone who offers a broad range of flexible options, significant socially responsible options, good online account access and reporting, and lower fees.

- *Plan Administrator.* The plan administrator sets up the benefit structure and plan information, and tracks to make sure money is properly put in the right accounts. The company also provides IRS and ERISA reporting. Look for someone who has lower and transparent fees (or is willing to negotiate for lower fees), is easy to reach, is organized, and provides updates on the plan as needed. Administrators can guide you through what is needed to develop a plan and what needs to be distributed to employees and the government per law.

Taking the time to find a good and trustworthy financial advisor is key to developing the rest of the plan, so interviewing a few options is well worth the time. The advisor should offer recommendations on finding the best type of retirement plan, money manager, and plan administrator and guide your leadership through the process of developing a plan that is the best fit for your organization.

Your plan also needs at least one person within the organization to serve as a trustee of the retirement plan. It is likely the Executive Director. The plan also must be approved by the Board of Directors before going into effect, as the board has fiduciary responsibility for the organization.[8]

A considerable amount of work goes into setting up an independent plan, but once it is off and running, it is not difficult to maintain. If your organization is financially stable, will grow, and has the resources to do so, an inde-

pendent plan might make a lot of sense.

Employer Retirement Contributions

An employer contribution for each employee shows the organization's commitment to its employees' long-term future.

> The purpose of offering a retirement benefit is to force (rather help!) employees to save for retirement. There are many young people staffing small nonprofits who feel the significant burdens of student loans and credit card debt and delay retirement savings until that debt is paid, which could be more than 10 years down the road.

Should your organization offer a retirement contribution? A matching contribution? Or both?

At minimum, make an employer contribution for each employee instead of requiring a match. Matches tend to be used by the most financially stable staff and least used by those most in need of retirement savings. A contribution will ensure that all staff will have some savings.

Another option is to consider offering a combination of a contribution and a match. It will encourage some employees to add their own contributions sooner, which can grow significantly in the future. IWJ offers a five percent employer contribution plus an additional two percent match. This arrangement has spurred some employees to kick in their own two percent contribution to get the match, which can be a huge benefit to those employees upon retirement.

And how much should your nonprofit contribute? As much as possible! But again, it's something that could start small and increase over time. The smallest amount to administer a simple IRA program is two percent of compensation. Safe harbor 401(k)s require three

8. *www.dol.gov/ebsa/publications/ fiduciaryresponsibility.html*

percent of compensation. Depending on your plan structure and budget ability, consider starting at two–three percent and increasing one percentage point every year until you reach the level where you would like to be.

Information on workers' compensation and disability insurance can be found in Section 3, Chapter 2 on page 81.

Unpaid Benefits

There are many ways to provide benefits to employees that don't have additional budget implications for your organization. Some of these benefits can be just as valuable as health care and retirement, so give considerable thought to the following as a part of your policies.

Time Off (Vacation, Holidays, Sick, Maternity/Paternity Leave)

Your organization must have a policy within its personnel handbook/union contract on time off. Several years ago a small nonprofit had neither a vacation policy nor timesheet requirements for its sole employee. When the employee left, he said that in three years he never took a vacation day. He claimed back pay for six weeks vacation, which left the organization without enough funds to hire a full-time replacement. When the current director of the same organization (which eventually rebounded and hired someone new) was asked if the group had a vacation policy since that hurtful experience, she said "no, but we should."

Small nonprofits often see personnel policies as an administrative burden or as micro-management of employees in a small shop. Trust needs to be high, and so informality often rules the day. But when things go bad, policies protect the organization and provide structure and equity for everyone.

Vacation

All nonprofits can offer a good vacation policy. Your policy should consider the following:

- Give a generous amount of time, and encourage longevity by increasing vacation based on seniority. Consider giving full-time employees at least 15 vacation days the first and second years, 20 days the third and fourth years, and 25 days after five years of employment. Part-time employees should receive the same proportion based on the percentage of full time that they work.

- Be sure to set up an accrual system so that new staff can't take all his/her vacation right away and leave before it is earned. For example, a 15-day vacation benefit in the first year would accrue 1.25 days a month. A supervisor can make exceptions but should not allow too much deficit in case someone leaves before the rest is earned.

- Give vacation in half- and full-day increments. It is an administrative headache to do it by the hour, and who takes one hour of vacation?

- Establish limits on how many vacation days can be carried over from year to year. **Staff should be encouraged to take vacation every year and actually be on vacation when the time is being used.** This is useful for the individual, the work, and the organization. A reasonable amount is to allow people to carry over 10 days (or two weeks vacation) a year. Some organizations also have a maximum accrual before vacation time is required to be taken or lost.

- Clarify what happens when someone leaves. Check your state's Department of Labor to see what the wage payment laws are in your state. Be clear if employees will be paid for accrued but unused vacation time, and if the employee has to pay back vacation used but not accrued upon termination of employment.

In order to keep track of vacation days used and the accrual of vacation days, you need to have timesheets for all staff to record the information.

Holidays
The number of holidays offered to all staff depends on the work of your organization as well as the generosity of the vacation policy.

Some organizations opt to offer 10 days vacation but then close at the end of December–beginning of January, thus giving the equivalent of 15 days (three weeks) vacation. This doesn't work so well for organizations that have a religiously diverse staff, so a greater number of individual days given would provide greater flexibility. Some organizations also offer a couple of extra religious holidays to enable staff to celebrate sacred days within their own faith traditions.

Another common practice in small nonprofits is to make Election Day a holiday to encourage employees to participate in the democratic process. Staff, regardless of individual political affiliation or beliefs, is encouraged to be politically active and to volunteer in some way for the presidential or other elections.

Finally, employers sometimes ask employees to take holiday time off after the actual holiday. In many nonprofits, the end of December is a busy time for fundraising and receiving last-minute gifts from donors who want a tax deduction for that calendar year.

Staff work during the day on New Year's Eve to receive those calls/emails, but don't lose the benefit of a holiday by being able to take it later.

Paid and Unpaid Sick Time

Paid Sick Time
Paid sick time is a strong way to reflect the values of self-care and family care for an organization's employees. There are currently 40 million Americans without paid sick leave, which means that many people are coming to work sick or are unable to stay home to care for their ill family members.

> Nonprofits should allow employees to use paid sick time when he or she is ill, needs to consult a doctor, or has to be home when there is sickness in the family. Many organizations offer full-time employees 10 sick days a year, with part-time staff receiving a percentage of days.

Just like vacation time, it's best to accrue sick time by pay period, allow use in half-day or full-day increments, have a policy on the number of days that can be carried over to the following year, and stipulate what happens when an employee leaves. Usually unused sick time is not paid to the employee upon completion of employment. Place a cap on the number of sick days that can be accumulated. If you have a disability insurance policy, consider coordinating the two policies for continuous leave and as much coverage as possible.

Providing paid sick time shows that the organization that provides time for an employee to care for him/herself and family values a work/life balance. The organization also benefits. Sick employees who stay home are therefore not spreading germs to others in the office; in addition, folks who try to work when sick usually are not very productive and turn in lower-quality work. Healthier employees can also potentially yield lower health care costs. Many health care companies consider wellness visits and preventive services used by employees when calculating costs, which can lead to lower premiums.

Unpaid Sick Leave

Although the Family and Medical Leave Act (FMLA) is not required for private-sector employers with fewer than 50 employees, it is a good model to provide the same benefit for smaller organizations when the need arises. The government website describes FMLA as "designed to help employees balance their work and family responsibilities by allowing them to take reasonable unpaid leave for certain family and medical reasons. It also seeks to accommodate the legitimate interests of employers and promote equal employment opportunity for men and women.[9]"

FMLA is an unpaid leave for up to twelve weeks a year, but the employee keeps health care and is able to return to the job at the end of the period. It is to be used for the birth or adoption of a child, to care for a sick immediate family member, and to take medical leave when an employee cannot do his/her job.

Maternity/Paternity Leave

The laws regarding maternity leave in the United States are shameful. The United States is the ONLY advanced economy that fails to provide some kind of paid leave to new parents. There is no federally required paid maternity or paternity leave, and the unpaid leave covered by FMLA (see above) is only required by employers with more than 50 staff. There is a certain irony in asking a parent, with a new member of the family that has new expenses, to forgo pay for 12 weeks.

Too many parents go back to work after two weeks, or four weeks, or six weeks, which can often be too soon.

> Parents should not be punished for having children; instead they should be celebrated, given time to heal and adjust to lack of sleep, and bond with their new baby!

Therefore, employers should develop a policy that packages a 12-week paid maternity leave. This is an area where nonprofit organizations can be models of supporting women and families in the workplace. This policy is very important for future job recruitment, hiring, and the organization's long-term vision.

The least expensive maternity leave plan would be to offer six weeks paid maternity leave plus short-term disability. Many short-term disability policies consider giving birth to a child an eligible condition for disability. The leave would not be 100 percent paid on disability, but vacation time could be used to make up the difference.

Employees who work more than 30 hours a week are eligible for short-term disability. Many carriers provide 60 percent of pay for six weeks (vaginal delivery) or eight weeks (C-section). There is a 15-day elimination period before the disability insurance kicks in. So in practice this means an employee would use:

- 3 weeks on paid maternity leave (paid at 100 percent)
- 6 weeks short-term disability (paid at 60 percent)
- 3 weeks on paid maternity leave (paid at 100 percent)

Employees can also use any vacation time after the leave if additional time is needed. Encouraging employees to use paid sick time for maternity leave coverage is not recom-

---

9. *www.dol.gov/whd/fmla*

mended, since parents need to have adequate coverage in the event they or their children get sick.

Another option would be to offer 12 weeks paid maternity leave. In some places, it might make sense to offer the 12 weeks over the course of the first year of the child's life, so that the time away from the office can be staggered. Time could be used in one- or two-week increments so that it doesn't become additional vacation time. It would still be incredibly helpful to a new parent adjusting to a baby's needs.

Paid paternity leave should be provided, and new dads should be encouraged to take it. Strong dads lead to strong families – a value that employers should help support and nurture through a generous paternity leave policy. The statistics for this generation of parents shows large numbers of dual-income households and more equitable divisions of labor of housework and childcare. Greater numbers of men with children help make meals, change diapers, and play with their kids.

Parents who adopt a child should also be able to use maternity and paternity coverage.

Some directors and board members consider maternity benefits too high a cost. If every employee took advantage of this policy at the same time, it would indeed be quite expensive. However, the fact of the matter is that the average American parent has only two children, so in many workplaces it would not be used very often. Having a generous policy will attract strong talent and help retain a staff worth investing in. Moreover, the value of supporting good employees and strong families through a generous policy should be worth the potential cost.

Other Time Off

There are a few other types of time off that provide different benefits to the employee and organization.

Jury Duty. Encourages citizens to participate in the justice system and not be penalized for that responsibility. Some states require employers to pay employees for jury duty, so be sure to check your state Department of Labor website to make sure your organization abides by the law.

Funeral Leave. Promotes strong families and time spent with loved ones during difficult periods of life. Some organizations provide three to five days of funeral leave a year if needed.

Sabbatical/Professional Enrichment Benefit

Much of an employee's daily work is a whirlwind, with the employee reacting to crises, responding to e-mails, entrenched in the day-to-day operations of the organization. Employees who demonstrate longevity and commitment can be rewarded and encouraged to take a sabbatical. This opportunity supports the organization in a different way, encouraging the staff member to think about the big picture and complete a project that is mutually beneficial to the person and the organization.

The employee should write up an application that includes a proposal of how a paid leave will advance the organization's mission and enhance the employee's ability to do his or her job. This application could be for research, writing, training or travel purposes, as there are likely a number of different projects could benefit both parties.

Typically, a sabbatical is offered to employees who have been with the organization between five and ten years. The leave can vary, but is typically between 8–12 weeks. The employee's pay and benefits continue during this period.

An employee is often asked to stay with the organization for at least a year after his/her return from the sabbatical. And leave is usually lost if it is not taken during the year that the employee is eligible.

This important longer-term strategy on staff retention provides an opportunity for staff with significant history to contribute to the future of the organization. And actually three months isn't too long in the life of an organization, but it can be significant to energize an employee with time and space to focus on a project that can have benefit to the organization as well as other staff.

Flexible Time/Telecommuting

A generous flextime/telecommuting policy can be a key way to build a strong nonprofit. There are three main reasons why:

- *Higher staff retention.* At Interfaith Worker Justice, there are three women (other than its founder) who have been on staff for more than 10 years. The common thread? All are mothers to young children and they all work varying part-time schedules. The women have found an environment where they can work some days from home, leave work early to pick up their kids, and have flexibility when it is needed. Having a job that provides income for the family, that gives working mothers a way to contribute to society, and that is flexible and supportive of a work/life balance is a huge benefit to any employee.

- *Better productivity.* Working from home or at odd hours requires a certain amount of discipline that not everyone has. But for

some, it can yield better and more productive work. The parents mentioned above have to balance multitasking, delegation, project management, and efficiency both at home and in the workplace.

- *Happier staff.* Working from home means no commuting, and no gas or train card. Folks can create a pleasant work environment at home, and many like the idea of working in their pajamas. This option helps with staff retention and helps the employer save time and money by not having to hire and train new staff.

However, flexible time should be done in a careful and cautious way. There are lots of stories circulating about flextime employees who stop doing much meaningful work and lack accountability for that work. All of this can lead to hard feelings and low morale in the office.

To start, develop a flextime/telecommuting policy that can be requested by employees who qualify and are specific to job position, performance, and experience within the organization. It is often easy to consider individuals' personal commitments when thinking about flexible time (especially working parents), but organizationally it is better to develop an equitable policy that is based on job responsibilities and time worked for the organization. It is particularly challenging for new employees to be successful telecommuters. It is difficult to build relationships and absorb the organization's culture and work if one is not in the office, at least at the beginning. But for employees who have appropriate tenure, are accessible, and can complete their work remotely, it can be an important benefit.

In terms of process, have the employee request flextime to his/her supervisor. However, the supervisor should get approval from the Executive Director on each individual case before making a decision. While these arrangements are made on an individual basis, the overall impact of having people working from home could make the office environment seem empty or difficult. The Executive Director should ultimately balance schedules to encourage a positive working environment.

Once flextime is requested, include a trial period, typically three months. Any new workplace perk should include a trial period, as it's hard to know whether or not it will work. Include an option for either party to stop the agreement at any time or at the end of the period if it's not working for either party. And then check in at the end of the trial to make sure the arrangement is working for everyone.

During the trial period, provide as much support as possible to make flextime easy and productive. Many folks have smartphones and laptops that can be used for work. But what about a way to access work files remotely? A Web-based database to have access to contacts? Or an extra license for software that helps the employee access his or her work from home?

The supervisor should also be clear about communication and availability during the flextime. For example, if an employee is going to work from home from 9 am to 5 pm on Fridays, it should be clear that the employee should be accessible throughout that time period, just as she would be in the office.

The flextime agreement should also be done in writing. A brief e-mail or letter should be written from the supervisor to employee with:

- Name of employee
- Supervisor approval
- Hours and schedule
- Communication expectations. Should she be available via e-mail and phone? When?
- Dates of trial period
- What files can be taken home and what can't
- What happens if it doesn't work out

The agreement should be printed out and put in the employee's personnel file. For Executive Directors, such requests should be made to the Board of Directors – either the Executive or Personnel Committees or the whole leadership.

Many nonprofits have found that offering flexible schedules has helped retain valuable employees. It can be a huge benefit to the employee and the organization to work together on scheduling and finding a solution that works for everyone – a win-win situation!

Chapter 4: Best Practices on Personnel Policies

There are a number of other procedures that don't need to be included in the personnel policies but promote an organizational culture of clarity, fairness, and transparency. The best practices selected below will help employees feel properly oriented, treated fairly, and, when they leave, supported and departing with good feelings and relationships with the organization.

Employee Orientation

Employee orientation is the first impression of your organization to any new staff. It provides the crucial context that folks need to understand the organization and their roles, as well as the practical information they need to do their jobs. Orientation should be handled consistently for all staff in the same way and should provide an abundance of information and suggestions for the new employee to get her footing.

Orientation Process

Because orientation can be overwhelming, it is good to have a process that allows the new employee to receive the information, process it, and meet with others who can help process it. Here's a sample process:

- **Orientation Meeting**. This is best led by the Executive Director or other senior staff. This provides an opportunity for the new person to start building a relationship with the director, and it also presents consistent information for each orientation session. It usually takes about 4 hours total (with breaks) to complete a thorough orientation.

- **Internal Meetings**. The new staff person should build relationships and start to understand and embrace the way the organization works. Depending on the responsibilities of the job, this could include the following:

  - Weekly check-in with supervisor for the first few months
  - Database training
  - Staff meeting
  - Board meeting
  - Volunteer or other membership or leadership meetings
  - One-on-one meetings with other staff (as many as possible)
  - Union officer (if have a union contract)
  - 1 month check-in with the Executive Director (or whoever did the orientation) for any outstanding orientation/personnel questions
  - Any other committee meetings or conference calls related to the organization that would be helpful to the person's job, especially those the new employee will be tasked to plan in the future! (event planning, phone banking, etc.)
  - Board member meetings. If you belong to a very small staff, you may ask several board members to help guide the new staff and give a sense of the organization's history and vision.

- **External Meetings.** The new staff should start meeting people in the community right away! Time to meet folks before diving into work will help the employee get to know people and get up to speed on the organization's programming and reputation in the community. Any public event hosted or featuring your organization such as workshops, classes, fundraisers, trainings, press conferences, coalition meetings, and meetings with donors can all be enormously helpful to a new person.

- **Training.** Usually, a new employee doesn't have all the skills he/she needs to do all aspects of the job. While learning through experience is one of the best ways to learn something at work, it can also be beneficial to get some formal training in areas where a bit of outside guidance would help the new employee do a better job. The employee's supervisor should talk with the new staff about where they feel least equipped to tackle the work, and talk through different training opportunities that might exist. This could include internal training with other staff, mentorship with senior staff or board members, free training, or paid training if the budget allows.

Paperwork

Inevitably, a number of forms need to be completed when an employee is first hired. It is a good practice to have all the paperwork completed and a personnel file started by the end of the first day. Basic forms for a new hire include:

- New Hire Form
  - Employee Name
  - Start Date
  - Position
  - Annual Salary
  - Full-time or Part time (number of hours per week)
  - Union position?
  - Eligible for benefits?
- Job Application Information
  - Candidate's resume, cover letter, references
  - Verification Form that attests the application information is correct
  - Job description for the position
- Payroll Forms
  - New employee info sheet (by payroll service or with info required by ac-

counting software)
  - Direct Deposit Form
  - Federal W-4
  - State W-4
  - I-9 Form
  - Copy of ID for I-9 Form
- Benefits
  - Acknowledgment Form of Benefits Info received
  - Enrollment package, summary plan description, and summary of benefits coverage for benefits offered by the organization such as health care or retirement.
    The Affordable Care Act also requires an employer to provide a Healthcare Marketplace notice, found at www.hhs.gov.
- Emergency Contact Form with an emergency contact name, relationship to employee, address, e-mail, work phone, and cell phone. This is a very important form to have on file.
- Acknowledgment Form of Staff Manual received
- Union Dues Authorization (if applicable)

Orientation Session

A common mistake made during orientation is not providing enough of the "big picture." Folks know where to find the pencils, but they don't understand the history of the organization. Most importantly, they don't understand how their work will help move the organization toward its mission. Below are the types of information that should be shared during an orientation.

- Organizational Overview (Big Picture)
  - History
  - Mission, Vision, Values
  - The role of the new employee/job in helping accomplish the mission

- Current Information on the organization (Little Picture)
  - Annual goals and objectives
  - Organizational Structure
    * Staff structure, explaining supervision and accountability, including Staff responsibilities
    * Board structure and board members
    * Other significant folks in the organization and how they work such as volunteers, workers, and members
  - Programs and which staff run which programs
  - Finances
    * Budget
    * Financial history
    * Fundraising, including where the money comes from and expectations related to the new employee to raise money
- The JOB! (Individual picture)
  - Job description and scope of work
  - Department or program goals (if they exist or are different from annual organizational goals)
  - Expectations related to other organizational involvement such as fundraising, managing volunteers, attending board meetings, running committees or events for the organization
  - Develop a three-month work plan
- Nuts and Bolts
  - Review employment forms (receive by end of first day)
  - Review union contract/personnel policy
    * Hours of work
    * Wages
    * Benefits
  - Additional organizational policies
  - Sign acknowledgment form in staff manual
  - Annual calendar dates such as staff retreat, staff meetings, board meetings, and holidays
- Office Administration
  - Office tour, including supplies, materials, and kitchen
  - Give keys and review access/security issues
  - Phone, voicemail, computer, and e-mail set-up
- Internal Procedures
  - Timesheets
  - Credit cards (if applicable)
  - Expense/reimbursement procedures
  - Travel procedures
  - Annual evaluation processes
- Next Steps
  - Scheduling meetings (outlined above in the evaluation process)
  - Reading
    * Staff manual
    * Organizational website
    * Other organizational publications, including newsletters, annual reports, and curricula
    * Anything else appropriate for the job, such as books, newsletters, magazines, and movies that might help
    * Subscriptions that would be helpful to the job, including online e-newsletters, e-mail lists, and professional publications

This will be a lot of information to process, so the supervisor and Executive Director should be available for questions in the first few weeks. A strong employee orientation helps new staff feel welcome and equipped to tackle the hard road ahead! It's well worth spending the time to develop an orientation agenda and staff handbook that can be updated and used for all those in the future.

Employee Exit Policies and Procedures

Employees come and go in the nonprofit world, often at alarming rates. This section provides some guidance on policies related to termination of employment (resignation and layoffs) and suggestions on procedures for those employees to exit in a responsible and thorough manner.

Exit Policies

Employees leave for three reasons: resignation, layoffs, and termination.

Resignation

Most personnel policies request that employees give between two and four weeks notice. This is a reasonable amount of time to wrap up work and provides a bit of transition if someone is hired quickly or moves internally. It is respectful to the organization for the departing employee to be diligent in organizing files and provide an exit memo on work before leaving.

Although there are some positions in which it is helpful to give a good deal more notice, the challenge is that many people find themselves mentally "out the door" once the resignation is announced. Thus, once an employee decides to leave, the supervisor and the employee should determine an end date that works for both parties.

A resignation notice from an employee should be written via e-mail or letter and placed in the person's personnel file. This makes a permanent record of the closing of the file and also protects the organization from any future issues such as ineligible requests for unemployment pay.

Finally, be sure to establish a process for submitting the final paycheck. If you have a policy of paying accrued but unused vacation days, just add them to the final check and pay it out in the person's last pay period.

Layoffs

Layoffs occur when an employer reduces staff positions altogether or eliminates a particular position. Layoffs usually occur to fix serious budget problems and are one of the hardest things faced by any nonprofit. Not only is it difficult to make the decision and follow through on it, but it can quickly lead to low staff morale and shaky financials.

Be sure to make the layoff process quick yet inclusive. Staff should be notified with at least two weeks notice. The Executive Director should document any notice of layoffs in writing, and the Executive Committee (or officers) of the Board should notified. In addition, a copy of the notice should be presented to each affected employee and put into the individual's personnel file.

In the event of layoff or reduction of hours, severance pay, if possible, can help with the individual's transition. How much depends on the budget, of course. Some common scenarios in small nonprofits are:

- Two weeks severance pay after last day of work
- One week severance pay for each year employed by the organization
- No severance pay, but continuation of health care benefits for two to three months after last day of work

Often employees qualify for severance pay if they have been employed by the organization for at least one year, after a probationary period and generally when someone is an established member of the staff.

Finally, be sure to keep the remaining staff informed on when layoffs occur, for what reason, and how these layoffs will provide needed financial stability so that it doesn't happen again anytime soon. Layoffs will inevitably lead to low staff morale, but it can also lead to panic and lots of folks looking for new jobs if it is not addressed in a respectful and informed manner. The director should provide leadership in this area by addressing the whole staff on this issue, orally and in writing, and offer an open door to anyone who wants to have a private conversation about why layoffs were in the best interest of the organization.

Termination

Some employees are not a good match for the organization and should not continue on as staff. Review Chapter 1 *Personnel Policies* for the disciplinary steps leading up to termination. Clearly written disciplinary procedures will guide the process up to the necessity of letting someone go.

However, once someone has gone through the progressive, multistep process of discipline, or has performed misconduct that violates your personnel policy, he/she can and should be terminated.

Termination should be done very thoughtfully, in specific detail, and in writing. An exit agreement should be drafted that details the reason for the termination, the steps that were taken to work with the person (with dates if possible) to fix the issue, and the details of the termination. Be sure to include what both parties agree to say and not say regarding the person's termination. A short timeframe is best as you don't want trouble brewing in the office that leads to staff drama later on A copy of the written document should be put in the employee's personnel file.

Some tips on thoughtful and fair procedures in employees leaving (regardless of reason):

- **Don't let the rumor mill get too big**. Whenever a person leaves, for whatever reason, folks start talking. Don't let gossip make a bad situation worse. If someone is being dismissed or laid off, do it in a timely manner, communicate with staff in a careful way, and offer to talk to folks privately if there are questions. Be very careful neither to publicly bad mouth a former employee nor to reveal confidential material from their personnel file.

- **Take charge of the messaging**. People leave for lots of reasons, some of which are not appropriately shared with all audiences. Talk to the person about what the message should be regarding his or her departure. Then, write an e-mail to staff (even if everyone clearly knows about it) explaining the transition, the formal reason for leaving, and what will happen next with the position. It will be helpful in getting everyone on the same page and providing information for staff to talk about the person leaving.

- **Communicate with the board on personnel issues, consistently and appropriately.** Although the Executive Director is responsible to hire and fire staff, he or she may choose to communicate with the board members who may be close to staff or serve as volunteers for the organization. Board members want to know what is happening with staff, so be sure to report on any changes as soon as possible in an official way. It also gives board members a heads up in case staff call board members for whatever reason. For example, a former staff member who resigned called the board chairperson to complain about the management of the Executive Director. The chairperson already knew about the situation and so was ready to support the director and minimize the drama that could have been created.

- **Encourage open and clear communication**. One staff person got an e-mail on a Friday afternoon that layoffs were to occur at the end of that following Monday. The staff endured the news over the weekend, and then the next week, every person was called into the conference room individually and told whether they were to stay or were laid off. What a terrible way to communicate a hard situation. Everyone wants to be treated respectfully in an open and fair environment. This doesn't mean that everyone needs all of the information. But it does mean that folks should be communicated with in a personal, direct, and consistent way.

Exit Checklist

When an employee leaves the organization, there should be a checklist of things the person and supervisor are responsible for to ensure a smooth transition of work and responsibility. Following is a suggested checklist for staff leaving the organization:

Exit Checklist

Task	Person Responsible
Verify that a formal termination letter has been submitted	Supervisor
Determine official end date	Supervisor, Employee
Request time summary for accrued vacation days	Supervisor
Inform bookkeeper of date to be removed from payroll (including any accrued vacation days)	Supervisor
Schedule exit interview	Supervisor (include employee and Executive Director)
Document notes from exit interview	Supervisor
Organize files and desk area	Employee
Prepare exit memos for each project	Employee
Schedule handoff meetings ○ Transition contacts ○ Hand over exit memo ○ Forward relevant e-mail ○ Organize information on computer/shared computer drive ○ Share all passwords with supervisor	Employee
(If appropriate) Notify contacts of departure and introduce successor	Employee
Return office keys, phone, laptop, and any other organization property	Employee
Submit forwarding contact information, including mailing address, phone number, and e-mail address to supervisor and Executive Director	Employee
Change employee's e-mail password, review and forward pertinent memos	Supervisor
Provide way to thank employee for his/her contribution (through card, small gift, snack at staff meeting, etc.)	Supervisor
Re-direct employee's e-mail account and phone voicemail to supervisor or successor.	IT person/director

An exit interview can be a helpful time for the employee and organization. It should be done by the employee's supervisor, and it is a time to review outgoing tasks as well as seek feedback and reflection from the employee on their experience and thoughts for the organization in the future.

Training and Professional Development

Fostering staff leadership should be a core value in the way your organization supports employees. Providing opportunities for continuing education and training is valuable for employees and builds a strong organization. It also shows an investment in staff, giving people the skills and training needed to successfully do a good job.

> The first step in professional development is having regular and good supervision so that employees are able do excellent work. Supervision is a year-round practice of checking in with employees, providing regular useful feedback, and encouraging training to address performance issues and promote professional growth.

Often supervisors are new at managing employees, so it's important to get some training on working with staff and supervising them effectively.

A formal opportunity for evaluation is done once a year. The employee's annual evaluation is a good time to discuss and reflect on the person's individual gifts and identify areas where training would be useful. Several types of training could be considered:

- *Regular Supervision*. The employee's supervisor should serve as support, advocate, and mentor to the employee.

- *Staff Meetings and Retreats*. The employee should have regularly scheduled opportunities to meet with other staff as a whole or in departments to discuss internal operations, policy, and programming of the organization.

- *Professional Literature*. Learning through reading is an important education for every employee, especially in small organizations where departments don't exist and often each person is expected to be the expert in her field.

- *Training*. Sessions exist on almost any topic imaginable from major donor fundraising to learning PowerPoint. Training always takes time, and very often it takes money, so employees should be careful to prioritize what training is important and seek approval to attend those first. In-person meetings provide opportunities for networking, but webinars or live Facebook chats can also be valuable tools.

- *Peer Exchanges*. Opportunities should be provided both within and outside of the organization for staff to connect with others that have similar responsibility and accountability in the organization.

- *Mentoring*. Many large corporations institute mentoring programs for staff to meet with each other from across departments for networking, strategizing, and mentoring from a more experienced staff. Small organizations, especially those with inexperienced staff, would also benefit from intentional mentoring from a board member, senior colleague in an allied organization, or other individuals with skills and experience that match the employee's training needs. Some of these programs are very simple. The two individuals meet once a month for an hour somewhere offsite to talk about what is important to the employee.

Chapter 5: Legal Matters

Even though employers want their staff to be happy and content in their jobs, the largest growing category of civil lawsuits in the country are employment-related cases. Therefore, nonprofit leaders must trust staff and make sure the organization is protected.

Employee Eligibility

Most personnel policies begin by stating who is covered. All employees should be covered by most of the policy, but it is tricky to offer the same paid benefits to all employees, regardless of hours worked and if someone has temporary or permanent employment. Therefore, it is useful to be upfront about eligibility for benefits to promote a culture of transparency and fairness.

> ORGANIZATION NAME offers benefits to permanent full-time and permanent part-time employees. Specific benefits are limited to those employees who qualify, which are indicated below.

Then name the job titles that do qualify, or a minimum of hours worked per week. Many policies stipulate that every permanent employee who works at least 20 hours a week qualifies for an appropriate portion of the benefits.

Disclaimers

Another consideration in developing a personnel policy is to make sure it has a disclaimer that the employee signs as part of staff orientation. This type of statement acknowledges that the person has received the handbook and understands that policies can and do change. An example of such a statement follows:

> This handbook reflects the organization's current policies and procedures. This handbook supersedes any prior handbook. The organization reserves the right to change these policies as needed.
>
> *By my signature below, I acknowledge and agree to the following: I received the organization's handbook and understand that this handbook does not constitute an employment contract. The organization reserves the right to depart from these policies when it deems it appropriate to do so.*
>
> _____ _____
> *Employee Signature*   *Date*

It sounds legal and maybe too much for small organizations, but this language will help protect the organization from legal misunderstandings with unhappy employees. It also clearly states that sometimes policies need to be changed and that the employee is always covered by whatever the current policies are, not the policies that existed when the person was hired. That is an important distinction which all employees should understand at the beginning of their employment.

For employees who are unionized, the collective bargaining agreement indicates eligibility of the contract conditions and benefits. It cannot be changed without union involvement in the process.

Employment Policies and Practices

There are federal and state laws that protect workers from discrimination in the workplace.

When hiring and recruiting staff, volunteers, or interns, it is very important that your organization not post jobs that discriminate or ask inappropriate and illegal questions. Your organization doesn't want to break the law, and it could ultimately lead to a job candidate filing an employment discrimination case against the organization.

In a job interview, the questions asked should be related to the job. Questions about skills, experience, and education are appropriate as they relate to the responsibilities outlined in the job posting.

> Questions that employers should not ask during an interview are those related to personal issues such as a candidate's age, race, gender, religion, marital status, disability, ethnic background, country of origin, or sexual preferences.

There might be some jobs, however, that require job-related questions in the areas above. For example, it would be appropriate to ask about a candidate's experience working with the Asian community, but not whether the candidate is Asian.

Personal questions are allowed as long as they relate to topics such as "things you do for fun." If the candidate brings up personal matters on his or her own, you can talk about it but should not encourage any information other than what the candidate provides.

If you are unsure about what is appropriate or not in employment hiring practices, consult the Equal Employment Opportunity Commission website at *www.eeoc.gov*.

Files

There's entirely too much paper in our professional lives. Even with the green movement's successful efforts in not printing e-mails, recycling used paper, and using double-sided printers, paper still abounds.

On the positive side, keeping thoughtful track of all of this stuff will help create institutional memory, protect your organization from potential personnel issues, and save you time when you need to find something!

With regard to personnel, the organization needs to keep the following documents:

- **Personnel File** (Permanent). A file for every current and former employee should be maintained and should include the following information:
    - Employment history, including employee name, start date, end date (if former staff), position, annual salary, full-time or part-time status and number of hours worked per week, if the position is union (if applicable). Be sure to include the job description with the position and any salary increase, hour changes, job changes, or changes in benefits.
    - Payroll forms such as the enrollment information for payroll service or the info sheet for accounting software, direct deposit form, federal W-4, state W-4, I-9, copy of ID for I-9.
    - Emergency Notification Form with contact information in case of an emergency, including name, e-mail address, phone number, address, and relationship to the employee.
    - Other authorization/acknowledgment forms such as:
        * Authorization of union dues if there's a contract
        * Signed acknowledgment that employee received the staff manual and understands the personnel policies.
    - Annual evaluation reports
- **Timesheet recording spreadsheets** (Permanent). This is not the timesheets themselves, but whatever tool is being used to record hours, vacation, sick, compensatory, and other paid time. This might be an Excel spreadsheet or recorded through

your payroll service.

- **Timesheets** (2 years). Keep the timesheets themselves for a while to make sure there's a record in case questions on hours arise.

- **Payroll register** (Permanent). Reports for each payroll, through either the service or accounting software.

- **Group Insurance Reports** (Permanent). These are the reports and coverage summaries for insurance, including workers' compensation, unemployment, short-term disability (if required by your state), and any other types of insurance the organization has.

- **Withholding Tax Statements** (7 years). These are W-2s. The accounting software or payroll service should have these on record pretty easily, as long as they have been given out every year!

- **Payroll Tax Returns** (5 years). Federal and state tax return reports, like form 941. You should have state tax returns for every state where you have employees working.

- **Retirement and Pension Records** (Permanent). The retirement plan description, funds descriptions, enrollment forms, and any other administrative information should be kept.

Chapter 6: Evaluation

Every employee within your organization should be evaluated regularly. Evaluation time presents an important opportunity to reflect with each person on accomplishments, challenges, future workplans, and professional development needs. The employee new to the job should be evaluated at six months, and all employees should regularly have an annual evaluation.

Six-month Evaluation

For a new staff person, a six-month evaluation provides a good check-in so the employee doesn't have to wait until the end of the year to be evaluated. In six months the employee should have learned about the organization and the work, gotten some experience in actually fulfilling the responsibilities of the job, and worked directly with others. The six-month evaluation is a good final step in an effective employee orientation. It can also mark the end of an employee's probationary period, if such a period is outlined in the personnel policy.

The evaluation should be a one-hour meeting scheduled between the employee and her supervisor. It doesn't have to be written, although if performance issues have cropped up, the evaluation should be written down. The supervisor should send out the following questions (and supervisor's answers if written) to guide the discussion at least a week before the meeting.

- What are your key accomplishments in the last six months?
- What have been some challenges in your work?
- How can your supervisor and others in the organization help you do your best?

- What are your goals and projected outcomes for the next six months?
- Are there any additional things you need to perform your job satisfactorily?

Annual Evaluation

Every employee should be evaluated on an annual basis by his/her direct supervisor. Ideally, this evaluation should take place before the end of the year that is being evaluated, so that training opportunities and work priorities can be included in the employee's following year work plan.

Much like the six-month evaluation check-in, the annual evaluation provides the employee and supervisor the opportunity to reflect on the employee's accomplishments and challenges for the year, get feedback on his/her work, give input into future work plans and priorities, make sure the job description is still up to date, and identify any training opportunities needed.

Evaluation reports and meetings shouldn't contain many surprises. It is the responsibility of the supervisor to informally raise any issues or change in work prior to the evaluation meeting. The evaluation provides more space to discuss the issue as well as discuss any solutions as needed. If major surprises come out of the evaluation, you and your supervisor should think about ways to communicate more in order to "nip it in the bud" before the end of the year.

Evaluation Process

It is helpful to have a written process not only for clarity's sake but also for the organizational history of future staff and board members.

Here's a sample process:

During the evaluation process, supervisors may review a staff member's work products and the results of relevant projects. Supervisors may also reach out to the staff member's colleague, and/or people outside the organization for additional feedback.

The evaluation process consists of three main steps:

1. The staff member completes a self-review and sends it to his/her supervisor. The staff member may choose up to two colleagues (within or outside the organization) to conduct colleague assessments. These assessments are sent directly from the person to the supervisor. The supervisor then drafts his or her review and sends it to the staff member.

2. The staff member and supervisor meet to review each section of the evaluation. At the end of the meeting, the supervisor summarizes any overarching conclusions and next steps.

3. The supervisor may edit the evaluation to reflect new information from the evaluation meeting. The supervisor's evaluation is placed in the employee's personnel file. If there are specific areas where quick improvement is needed, the supervisor and staff member will agree on a plan, track progress against it, and take any other appropriate actions.

As noted above, while this formal evaluation system ensures that supervisors and staff members engage in summary discussions about performance at least once a year, this process should not be a substitute for regular check-ins.

This process works because it:

• Provides several perspectives of evaluation from the employee herself, from colleagues inside or outside the organization, and from the supervisor. Many staff spend more time working with people *outside* the organization than within, so it is a more appropriate evaluation of their work to ask others for feedback.

- Is based on outcomes, not just skill sets. Everyone should be focused on getting work done and on being able to articulate what that work is.

- Connects the current year with planning for next year. The evaluation is a planning tool that should help significantly with the next year's planning.

- Has a focus on professional development and training. All have room to grow and should be encouraged to make improvements in doing the jobs.

The forms to accompany the evaluation process are a self-evaluation form, colleague evaluation form, and annual review form (which ends up in the employee's personnel file). None of the forms are complicated, but are intentionally left open for someone to provide more detail or raise some other concern if needed.

Job Descriptions

Every person on staff should have an accurate job description. The annual evaluation is a time to quickly check-in on the individual's job description and make sure it is up to date.

Job descriptions shouldn't be too detailed, naming every little task; rather, it should be an accurate summary of the major responsibilities for each staff position and skills required to do the job. Usually, the job description is written up when the position itself is being advertised.

Staff should look at their job description to reflect on their work for the year and make sure all the responsibilities are covered when developing work plans. The Executive Director should also review all the descriptions once a year and flag any discrepancies between theoretical and evolving job responsibilities.

One small nonprofit director once sought support from a mentor on how to approach firing a nonperforming staff member. The mentor told her to consult the job description for that position so that she could explain to the staff and board why the termination was happening. There was no job description for either the staff member or for the Executive Director herself granting the authority to hire, manage, and fire employees. Before the disciplinary process could even begin, the director had to develop job descriptions, but even then it was hard to insist that an employee had not performed his job when no one was defining exactly what the job was.

It is helpful for people to understand what they are responsible for doing and how this tool is used for accountability and evaluation. Work has a tendency to change slowly over time, so a review can bring up gaps that can be addressed.

One small nonprofit organization schedules annual employee evaluations in the fourth quarter of the year and then has a staff retreat in the first quarter of the new year. Each person is asked to update his/her job description for the upcoming year based on the previous year's work. The job descriptions are reviewed and discussed at the staff retreat and then reviewed by the board's Executive Committee. It has helped expand communications between staff and board, identify gaps when new staff are hired, and promoted staff accountability.

Executive Director Evaluation

The Executive Director should be evaluated by the Board of Directors on an annual basis. Supervising the Executive Director is one of the core responsibilities of the board and one that is often ignored or delayed. Often, the board doesn't really know what the director does all day. A thoughtful evaluation takes time and input from others. And if the director is basically good, the board doesn't feel that evaluation is a priority.

Even if your organization has a good director, evaluation provides an opportunity for the board to gain insight into the director's work, offer support to the leader, and suggest feedback/growth opportunities for the director. This process can also have a positive impact on the relationship between the board and the director, where the board acknowledges the director's hard work and leadership and sees avenues through which the board itself can support the director in the work.

Executive Director Evaluation Process

The board should adopt a policy on the Evaluation Process for the Executive Director. Here is a sample process:

1. Executive Director completes a self-assessment and sends to the Board Executive (or Personnel) Committee.

2. The Executive Director provides names and e-mail addresses for those who are to be invited to complete assessments of her/his internal and external work. The board or personnel committee chair could also call these folks for an interview:
   ○ Up to 3 staff colleagues
   ○ Up to 3 other peer colleagues familiar with the director's work outside the office (e.g. ally staff, funders, coalition partners, etc.)

3. The Board Executive Committee may add more peers to receive the assessment in addition to the Executive Director's suggestions. Also, each board member will receive a form with the option to evaluate the Executive Director.

4. Colleagues and board assessments are sent directly to the board president. The president then drafts the board's review and sends it to the Executive Director.

5. The Executive Director and Executive Committee meet at the year-end board meeting to review each section of the evaluation. At the end of the meeting, the Board President summarizes any overarching conclusions and next steps.

6. The board president may edit the evaluation to reflect new information from the evaluation meeting. The evaluation is presented to the full board for approval, and a big thanks is given to everyone for pitching in. The evaluation is placed in the director's personnel file.

Four forms accompany the evaluation process: Self Review, Colleague Review, Board Evaluation, and Annual Review Form (which goes into the personnel file).

 Tips to supervisors on how to run an effective evaluation session

Evaluation sessions can be challenging. Here are a few tips on how to run a productive and constructive evaluation:

- *Set the stage for a good meeting.* Supervisors should choose a location for the meeting that will not have interruptions. Give yourself plenty of time so the meeting isn't rushed or doesn't get finished. And be prepared. Provide the evaluation review in advance and have copies at the meeting so you can dive right in.

- *Be positive!!!* Start with the things someone does well before any critique. Every employee brings some good experiences, skills, and personal gifts to his or her work. Make sure these positive qualities are reflected in a sincere way in the evaluation process. Employees won't be willing to hear any criticism without some affirmation of the good things they do.

- *Keep surprises to a minimum.* If there are major performance issues, you should have talked with the employee about it already. Major problems shouldn't just be raised in an annual evaluation session. Employees will say that they could have fixed things sooner if their supervisor had talked to them about them. The conversation should recognize major areas of growth and focus on ways to make things better.

- *Don't raise every single little problem.* Focus on the major issues that are impeding the individual's work, and let some of the smaller things go. Your written report should also concentrate on the things you really want the person to work on. You don't have time to address everything in a one-hour meeting, and the person won't be able to hear all of your feedback anyway.

- *Don't give up on someone too quickly.* Assume that every staff person is worth having on staff because he or she has skills, experience, and personal gifts to bring to the position and that he or she is doing good work. Not everyone is equal, and some people do a better job than others. But every person on staff should get support from his/her supervisor, feedback on the work, plans for the future, and training.

The evaluation is not a disciplinary session. If you have a staff person who is not doing satisfactory work or is guilty of some kind of misconduct, the issues should be addressed through your organization's disciplinary procedures and the employee should be given the opportunity to fix the problem or leave the organization. The annual evaluation is not the time to put someone on probation. That should have been done already if there were problems. Don't let personnel issues fester: It's not good for the work, the individual, or one's colleagues.

Section 2

Board

Introduction

1. Roles and Responsibilities of the Board

2. Board versus Staff Roles

3. Expectations of Board Members

4. Role of the Executive Director to Help the Board Function

5. Composition and Structure

6. Meetings

7. Strengthening Your Board

Introduction – Leadership, Teamwork, Commitment

Organizations need many types of leaders including the Executive Director, other management staff, program leaders, volunteers, workers, and, yes, the Board of Directors.

Often, too much emphasis is placed on the leadership of the Executive Director, and not enough work is put into developing and strengthening the board.

A successful board has members that are committed to the mission of the organization, are leaders, and can work together well as a team. Board members bring a variety of skills, expertise, connections, and life experience to your leadership. This experience can be very useful in organizational growth and thinking outside of the box in so many areas.

A board safeguards the organization's resources. In one small organization, the board discovered that the Executive Director was putting personal expenses on the organization's credit card. More than $1,000 in donations were wasted because there was no process in place to review the expense reports.

A board ensures compliance with the law. A tax-exempt organization legally cannot exist without a functioning board, and operating without one can cause the organization to face legal troubles or loss of tax status. If you are just starting out, you can't incorporate your organization, apply for tax status or for funding without a board.

A board provides fiduciary oversight. Although you trust your staff, you shouldn't trust them too much. Directors and other staff can be tempted to steal, make contracts that are self-dealing, or misappropriate funds.

A board legitimizes your organization. At a recent meeting of church women, one of the participants presented a nonprofit organization for partnership and explained that the board was a diverse group of reputable, engaged, smart leaders (including one board member who used to lead her religious denomination). Connections, titles, and leadership positions all matter. A board of well-known, connected leaders from the community demonstrates the strength and effectiveness of your work.

A board shows that your organization is accountable in the community. It is especially important for community-based or worker-led organizations to have accountability for your work and input from those with whom you serve or work.

A board helps fulfill the mission (i.e., do the work!). Board members can meet with donors, do media interviews, attend actions, advise staff, and much more! Every board member should be doing something significant to help the organization. Otherwise why are they on the board?

A board recommends the organization to funders. Many grant applications require a board listing as part of the application, and some ask for addresses and phone numbers of board members in order to reach the leadership directly. Strong leadership is another way to show a strong organization that is attractive to funders whose support you want.

The chapters in this section provide tools that will strengthen board leadership. They clarify the appropriate roles between board and staff; lay out realistic expectations for folks who are often busy leaders; provide suggestions on structure and terms; and advise on how to make your board even better than it is now. The stronger the board is, the stronger your organization will be.

Chapter 1: Roles and Responsibilities of the Board

Regardless of an organization's structure, board members have significant responsibility as the leadership of an organization. Below are roles and responsibilities that should be carried out by volunteer board members and not staff.

Set Program Directions and Priorities

The Board of Directors develops the mission and vision of the nonprofit and reviews it periodically to make sure it is still relevant. The leadership should be in agreement on the vision of the work and purpose of the organization within that vision. A strong vision will attract new leaders to the work. This vision should be shared with new board members during orientation and through strategic planning with other board members, or at the end of every year when discussing next year's annual goals and objectives.

The board sets and approves the organization's annual goals and objectives. The big vision is great and inspiring, but it doesn't tell us how to create change. The board should review the annual goals and objectives (before the year begins!) and:

- Make sure that program work falls within the mission and vision.

- Make sure that the goals are realistic and that objectives are measurable and possible for the staff capacity and resources you have.

- Help propose new work that meets the mission and vision if necessary. This goal can be tricky, but the board has an important role to play in changing priorities. For example, IWJ's board in the aftermath of Hurricane Katrina proposed the creation of a new affiliate organization in New Orleans to support workers and protect worker standards as the community was being rebuilt. It required a significant revision of the organization's annual goals, but it was a strong show of leadership in reaction to a monumental national crisis.

The board approves the annual budget and fundraising plan. Once board members have seen the goals and objectives, they should review the proposed budget and fundraising plan. It is important to analyze how money is raised and spent, given the work plan. Board members should also ensure that the budget is realistic (given the work plan), fair, and balanced. Steps should be made to promote financial stability through developing a cash reserve fund. The reserve fund will provide a cushion when the budget is tight.

The fundraising plan should be reviewed to make sure it is realistic, diverse in sources, and that board members are involved. This is a good time to seek support for different fundraising strategies and make sure board members are making personal contributions.

The annual goals, budget, and fundraising plan are intertwined and heavily dependent on one another. If the work plan is too big for the money that will be raised, then it needs to be adjusted. If the fundraising plan is not as big as the budget, the budget needs to be lowered. Ambitious plans are good for motivation, but only if they are ambitious AND realistic. Goals or fundraising plans based on dreams set the staff up to fail at best, and at worst you run out of money.

Maintain Financial Integrity

The board has significant responsibility (and liability) with regard to finances. Yet, it's often an area that board members don't understand, don't like to talk about, or don't get enough information to make a good decision.

Board members, like everyone else, need training to do a good job. Financial training is an excellent way to start. There are lots of accountants who might be willing to do an hour session on the basics of how to read a budget, income/expense reports, and balance sheets. If possible, use your organization's financials in the training to get some real analysis and work done.

In addition to training, it's valuable to have some "money people" on the board. These folks should serve as your board treasurer or on the finance committee. Business owners, accountants, bankers, nonprofit executives, or anyone who works with financial reports regularly are good additions to a board. Don't give the money people all the power and decision-making, but use their advice and guidance to help the rest of the board understand what the financial priorities should be.

Review Financial Reports

The best way for boards to stay on top of the finances is to look at them all the time. The treasurer's report or finance and fundraising report should be a regular item on the agenda of every board meeting (and not the last!). Staff review reports should be gone over with the treasurer before the meeting, so that a board member is prepared to report to the full board. So the money conversation doesn't take over the meeting, give it a timeframe for discussion. As the board gets familiar with the reports and agenda, it does not need to take

more than 15 minutes unless there are serious issues that need to be addressed. Make sure the board gets the same reports again and again, so that it's easy to compare history and provide open and transparent information. Most boards look at the following reports:

Year to Date versus the budget versus prior year to date income/expense statement. These reports can be easily pulled from an accounting software program if the annual budget has been entered and bookkeeping is up to date. The board should look at reports that have been reconciled with the bank account, which means the reports might be a month or so behind. For example, if the board meets the first Tuesday of every month, the May meeting might not have records reconciled from April yet. The reports will likely have to be January–March of that year.

The basic information to look for in this report includes:

- Prior year versus year to date. Are there any major differences in income and/or expenses? What are they? Will they happen again?

- Year to date versus budget. Look at income and expenses separately.

  ○ Income. Is the fundraising on target? Staff should report back on progress related to the fundraising plan and check whether there are any significant differences with the plan. If so, how will the board adjust to those changes? Reduce spending? Increase fundraising efforts and/or personal gifts?

  ○ Expenses. Are there any major differences between actual expenses and budgeted expenses? If so, how does the board address those changes?

Balance Sheet

The balance sheet is a bit more complicated than the income/expense report. Make sure to have a "money person" around to ask questions if needed. But there are a few key items to review for board members:

- Account balances. How much cash is in the bank? Figure out how much cash is on hand. It doesn't take long to do a rough calculation of the organization's average monthly expenses and divide by the amount of cash in the bank. For example:

  - Organization spends $7,500 a month for payroll, benefits, rent, telephone, and other regular expenses
  - Bank account balance is $56,000
  - $56,000/$7,500= about 7.5 months

- Liabilities. Of course, this assumes you don't have much debt to worry about. So take a look at the liabilities section of the balance sheet and make sure it's not too high. Liabilities are the things that the organization owes, in both the short term and the long term. Make sure all the payables (things that are owed) are entered into the books, so that it shows up in the balance sheet. For example, if you haven't paid your rent for six months, it won't show up on your income/expense statement (except that you will be way under budget on rent) but it will show up on your liabilities. See if your cash can cover what is owed. If not, the organization is living close to the edge.

  Many small nonprofits only have a month or so of cash in the bank. This causes concern when making sure everyone is paid on time. The board should lead in setting a goal of having at least six months cash reserve and a plan to reach that amount to strengthen the organization.

Cash Flow Report

This statement is a monthly look at the cash coming into the organization and being spent each month. If your budget is small and you have consistent and reliable funding sources, you may not need this report. But you want to make sure you have enough money in the bank to meet your expenses. It is possible to bring in more income than expenses over the course of the year but still not have enough cash to pay the bills. Grants often send checks months after approving the funding. Having a reserve fund can help with cash flow, but only if you are able to replenish the reserve later and you aren't spending that money! This report is available in accounting software programs, but a manually prepared report might be more useful to see the future cash projections based on the fundraising plan. A sample report can be found in the finance section of this handbook.

If there's no problem with cash, the board may not need to regularly review this report. The balance sheet shows account balances, so it's easy for board members to see big variations in dollars in the bank. However, this tool is crucial for Executive Directors and other senior leadership to develop and manage. Many times folks can't see when cash flow problems are coming, as a result of which they don't have time to make adjustments or fundraise more before money runs out.

Other than the regular review, it's helpful to do a more thorough finance/fundraising check halfway through the year and at the end of the year. The midyear check-in allows the organization to see if there are any significant gaps while there's still time to launch fundraising that might help cover any problems. The end-of-the-year report is a good time to project the year-end finances and use that information to make a budget for the following year.

If you serve on a board and the staff does not provide financial reports, you should be worried. One consultant assumes there is thievery if the board is not given financial reports in two or more consecutive meetings. Board members don't get the tools they need to make good decisions when the organization's operational systems are disorganized.

File Financial Reports

The board is responsible for reviewing and approving the annual audit and IRS 990 tax form. If your organization isn't big enough for an audit (and this depends on your state, often based on income), hire an accountant to look at your books at the end of the year and provide a letter of financial review. The accountant should be a third party that doesn't have anything to do with your organization during the year.

The Form 990 should be filed every year. There are a few versions of the form on the IRS website, depending on your income. Some versions of the form are more complicated than others, so give yourself plenty of time to figure out which form you need and its requirements. The full 990 form asks about a number of internal policies (whistleblower, for example) that will take time to develop if they aren't already in place. There are federal and state versions of the form. You might consider having the accountant file the forms for you, but it's very possible to do internally by staff or the board. The penalty for not filing the form is very high: You could lose your tax-exempt status if you don't file. It is also a public document, which means it can be found easily on sites such as *www.guidestar. org* and it is looked at by funders, donors, allies, and enemies to check the state of your organization.

Planning Your Financial Future

The board should take the lead in thinking about the financial future of the organization. Board members should agree about what is important to spend money on and about plans for future spending and saving so that the organization is as financially healthy as possible.

For the budget, the most important place to start is to establish a cash reserve fund. It's your organization's savings account for when cash is tight or when the economy is bad. IWJ has a board policy of allocating 5 percent of the budget into a reserve fund. The organization is not always successful in putting away the full amount, but it is put into the budget as an expense account and most years some is socked away into the reserve. Every bit helps, and it will grow over time.

The financial future also means thinking about long-term fundraising. Many organizations are heavily dependent on grants. One organization shared the information that it had just lost a grant that represented a third of their budget. That is a dangerous and insecure way to operate. Start building long-term fundraising strategies that can grow over time, even though they may not have big short-term rewards. Many nonprofits need to build an individual donor base (or a database of folks if not done already!), start a major donor program, and generate grassroots support from the community. Start small and try to build on those efforts. It will pay off eventually if staff and board are committed, organized, and doing it consistently.

Raise Money

Board members give in many significant ways to help a nonprofit and a cause they care about. They give time, in-kind contributions such as services and free space, and buy things for the organization. But all board members need to give and raise money too.

In order to raise money, board members should first make their own personal, significant contribution. People have different abilities to give, so it's not about a particular dollar amount, but about giving at a level that is meaningful for each person. It's also really hard to raise money if one hasn't given yet. Funders also like the idea of 100 percent board giving, as it shows financial investment in the organization.

> All board members can reach out to their family, friends, neighbors, and communities to help raise money. The key is finding the best ways for as many board members as possible. Here are some ideas:

- *Add names of friends and family to the mailing list.* Write personal notes once a year to those friends asking to give, and follow up via e-mail or phone to encourage giving (this is great for the end of the year).

- *Hold a fundraising event.* It doesn't have to be fancy and expensive. With the right speakers and marketing, a breakfast or picnic or wine tasting can draw folks. Help with logistics and ask for support at the event.

- *Sell stuff.* Board members can sell tickets, sell ads for the ad book, or sell tables/sponsorship to organizations (law firms, corporations, vendors, schools, religious groups, unions)

- *Meet with donors in person*, especially major donors.

- *Find organizational sources of support,* such as corporations or foundations. Take the leadership to meet with program officers and encourage funding.

Board fundraising is absolutely crucial to meeting the budget and building the organization. If your board is not already helping to raise money, it needs to start doing so right now. Everyone should help, regardless of the amount of money that an individual or family gives in support. Building a culture of fundraising on the board (and staff too!) will keep people invested in the organization, bring more money in, and ensure that the money is spent responsibly.

Provide Leadership on Policies and Staff

Set Personnel Policies

It is the board's responsibility to set personnel policies for the organization. The staff can draft the organization's policies or negotiate the union contract, but the board should review and approve it. Many organizations also review their policies every two to three years, or as requested by staff to make adjustments.

If there are few policies currently in place, the board should direct the staff to provide a draft of policies for review, and quickly. There are many folks running organizations informally and in a spirit of trust and collaboration, so many basic policies have not been developed. In good times, there isn't much motivation to develop new policies. However, it only takes one complaint or messy staff transition to show the weaknesses of the organization's policies. In some cases, these deficiencies have led to the organization's closure.

One nonprofit had no clear policies on compensatory time for professional staff. When one director left the staff, he claimed he was owed six months worth of comp time, and so the organization ended up paying him six months of salary when he departed. Lacking clear policies proved very costly.

Good policies also fundamentally promote an organizational culture of transparency and respect for its employees. Worker justice organizations push employers to establish and abide by policies that treat workers with dignity and fairness. What example do those organizations set if they're not doing the same?

Creating personnel policies does not have to be a big project. Ask to see the policies of allied organizations and draft your own based on others' samples.

Hire the Executive Director

The Executive Director is supervised by the Board of Directors, so when the position is empty, it is the board's job to hire a new director.

A director transition provides a good opportunity for board members to:

- Assess the work of the organization and identify the strengths and weaknesses of the current work.

- Identify the experience, skills, and style needed by the new director, given the work of the organization.

- Develop a job description that articulates those qualifications, responsibilities of the job, and other requirements. (There are many examples of job descriptions at *www.idealist.org*.)

- Review and revise the search process to hire a director as needed.

Unless you have a very small board, form a personnel committee to lead the search. Sometimes the committee brings a recommended candidate to the entire board; other times, the committee brings several candidates for the board to consider. Also, think about having some kind of staff involvement during the director search process. Staff members, especially those who have been with the organization a long time, may offer a helpful perspective on choosing new leadership.

It can be beneficial to promote from within the organization. If the organization is in good shape with strong leadership, decent finances, and ambitious vision and programming, it's likely partially due to the efforts of someone who is already involved in the work. A new voice and perspective can be helpful, especially for dramatic transitions (rapid growth or change in direction), but internal promotion provides a career path for a current leader (staff, board, or volunteer) and requires much less training, which keeps the organization's work moving.

Evaluate the Executive Director

One of the biggest complaints from Executive Directors about their boards is that the board doesn't give them feedback on their work (the other big complaints are they don't do enough fundraising and don't provide enough leadership). We all want feedback on our work, concrete suggestions on how to be better, and opportunities for growth.

If the board thinks the director is good, it may not evaluate her because it doesn't seem important to do. But even good directors need evaluation. The board doesn't see the full picture of the work of its leader, and so an evaluation can provide feedback and also show how the director is spending her time. Does she need to consider workload, or prioritization of tasks?

If the director is struggling, the board may avoid evaluating her because it could cause tensions between the director and board. New and struggling directors need board support the most, and there should be members on the board who can help. In cases where the director is clearly not working out, the board needs to be able to show specifically where the director is not performing or has shown misconduct. The evaluation provides an important opportunity to start that conversation and be clear about what needs to be improved.

A suggested process on how to evaluate the Executive Director can be found in the staff section (Section 1) of this handbook.

Serve as a Grievance Committee for Staff

Your organization's personnel policy or union contract should have a grievance process. This is a way that an employee can raise a formal complaint against the organization's policy or a supervisor's interpretation of the policy.

This area of board work can be tricky and can easily create tension within the organization if it is not handled carefully. So be sure to have a very clear, multistep grievance policy in your organization's personnel policy. Be explicit about what kind of information needs to be written down, who will respond to the complaint, and in what timeframe.

If there is more than one staff person, the Executive Director should handle the grievances. The board should not get involved unless the director asks for help. If the grievance is against the Executive Director, the staff should approach the board Executive Committee or personnel committee.

The board should develop an ad hoc personnel committee (or have the Executive Committee/officers serve as the personnel committee). It shouldn't involve the whole board, as that increases the likelihood of drama and gossip within the organization. This committee can address grievances and periodically

review the organization's personnel policies as needed.

Set Guidelines for Staff (especially on money issues)

Although the board should not be involved in the day-to-day operations of the organization, policies and procedures should be set to make sure staff follow expectations of transparency, accountability, and ethical behavior within the organization. If someone steals from the organization, the board shares responsibility in allowing that to happen.

> The board sets the culture of the organization. Many other parties (banks, foundations, vendors) won't ask for a board member signer on major contracts, but you should insist on it internally as a way of promoting responsibility and engaging your leadership in organizational decisions.

A few examples of guidelines:

- Money-Handling Policies. You should consider setting a few key policies on how money is received and spent. For example, don't let the person who cuts the check sign the check above a specific amount (like more than $100). Have two check signers above a larger amount, maybe including the board treasurer. Also, make sure cash is kept secure, counted by two people when received, and recorded in a written document.

- Legal Contracts. Significant long-term commitments made by the organization should be signed by the Executive Director and Board representative (the President, in most cases). This forces information to be shared and verifies that more than one person has the responsibility to make commitments. Contracts for a database program, mortgage, or leases for office space are all significant contracts.

- Organizational policies that promote the culture of the organization. This could include a dress code policy to set expectations of how the organization should be represented, or travel guidelines on what is appropriate business expenses to promote a culture of responsible stewardship and thrift.

Make only the policies you need and make it easy for staff to follow the policies.

Set Policies and Procedures for the Board of Directors

Your organization's board should also develop and adhere to policies regarding itself. Some common board policies include:

- Expectations for board members. Board members should set and distribute expectations for what it means to be on the board. In what ways are all board members expected to contribute to the organization (yes, all board members need to fundraise!)? It is hard to ask board members to do something if they didn't know it was expected of them in the first place.

- Annual meetings/retreats. Board members decide how often they meet, when, and how long, and whether to hold any annual retreats or gatherings during the year.

- Self-assessment and evaluation. Boards should take some time to evaluate themselves and reflect on what works and doesn't work in the way the board runs the organization. This review could be done every year or two.

- Directors and Officers Insurance. Many board members won't serve on the leader-

ship team without this insurance. Review the insurance section of this book to learn more about this insurance and why it's important.

Assure Legal Compliance

It is the board's job to make sure the organization is meeting all of its legal obligations. Nonprofit organizations have a responsibility to model the kind of society internally that many diligently work for outside of the organization. Many groups also have enemies looking for weaknesses to stop the work so can't allow any gaps in the ways they run.

An easy way to make sure the organization is legally up to snuff is to have people on the board who have experience and/or interest in legal compliance. But generally speaking, the board has the following legal responsibilities:

- Make sure the activities of the organization are charitable and within its mission. Nonprofits are tax-exempt and receive that status by the government in order to conduct educational and charitable activities. The board is responsible for making sure the organization is following the law.

- Make sure money is used and raised honestly. Sometimes mistakes are made, but there is less legal trouble if the board can show that sound thinking and process was the basis for the decision and that the decision was made by people without a personal interest.

- Make sure no one is benefiting inappropriately from the organization. Board members should sign a conflict of interest statement that demonstrates individual and business interests held by board members. Board members should be volunteers and should be doing this service out of their commitment to the work. There are many stories in the news about personal use of public funds; the punishments are stiff for that violation of the law.

Represent the Organization

There are many opportunities to help the organization with outreach. Board members should be able to help represent the organization in public and speak to the issues. Some board members might not be good doing media interviews, but they are in the main excellent bloggers, social media writers, and letters to the editor writers. Some board members might speak or pray at rallies or emcee events. Others might be good trainers and want to do workshops or speak at conferences. Board members who speak other languages might help diversify your outreach speaking on radio programs or writing in newspapers.

Representing the organization also means connecting the organization to each board member's community. Individuals represent many different communities. Age, gender, religion, ethnicity, activism, all of these aspects of communities can be aligned with your work. Those appropriate representations should be brought into the nonprofit organization. For example, if your organization works with youth, young people should have a voice at your leadership table and be able to help connect the organization with youth in your community.

This sounds like a lot of responsibility. Well, it is! Board members are the leadership of the organization, performing a job (albeit unpaid) that should not be taken lightly.

Chapter 2: Board versus Staff Roles

Boards and staff need to work as a team. The roles may change somewhat over time, but leadership should be balanced between the board and staff. A common problem within nonprofits is clarifying the difference between board and staff roles. Here are some important distinctions between board and staff:

Program and Priorities

The board is responsible for the big picture and the staff is responsible for the day-to-day implementation of programs. The board is responsible for strategic planning and for requiring the staff to provide regular updates on the organization's programming.

Staff members need to draft and provide background materials for board members so they can make thoughtful leadership decisions. Staff can recruit board members to help with programming in many different ways, but they are in charge of making sure the annual goals are completed.

Maintain Financial Integrity

Both board and staff should be trained and equipped on basic financial management and fundraising. This shouldn't be a responsibility shared only by the board treasurer, chairperson and executive director. The more hands on deck, the more money will be raised!

Staff should work to provide consistent and regular financial, fundraising, and budget reports to the board. They should also take the time to develop strong systems so that they can manage money better and ensure that the board can see the complete financial picture at any one time. Board members should be observant and thoughtful in reviewing the budget and financial reports. Board members can help ensure that the budget stays in check and should ask questions when there are fuzzy numbers.

Both board and staff should be heavily involved in fundraising. Board members can do

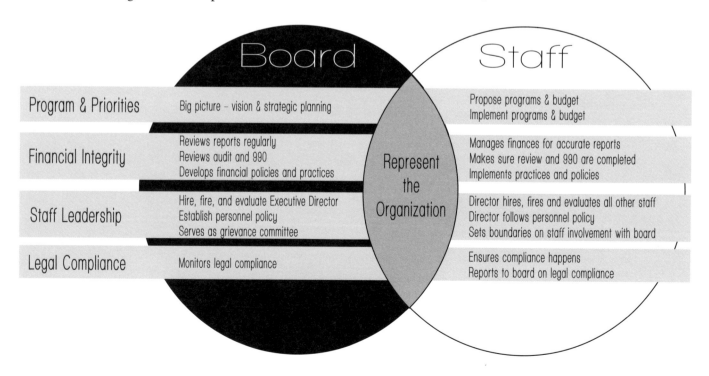

	Board	Staff
Program & Priorities	Big picture – vision & strategic planning	Propose programs & budget Implement programs & budget
Financial Integrity	Reviews reports regularly Reviews audit and 990 Develops financial policies and practices	Manages finances for accurate reports Makes sure review and 990 are completed Implements practices and policies
Staff Leadership	Hire, fire, and evaluate Executive Director Establish personnel policy Serves as grievance committee	Director hires, fires and evaluates all other staff Director follows personnel policy Sets boundaries on staff involvement with board
Legal Compliance	Monitors legal compliance	Ensures compliance happens Reports to board on legal compliance

Represent the Organization

many things to raise money, like meet with donors, give names of friends, and connect staff with new foundation or corporate contacts. Board members should be involved in fundraising in a way that makes it *easier* for staff to raise money. Big events, in particular, can be popular and profitable, but also a huge burden for staff. Board members should be very careful in making budget decisions and need to spend money wisely.

Staff should develop and implement the budgeting process and fundraising plan. So it is their job to organize the board to make sure all board members are involved in specific fundraising tasks and that it is easy for board members to do their part. Staff have the responsibility of recommending budget revisions or fundraising ideas to the board but have to be careful to prioritize what is possible with limited resources and time. Staff should also identify what they can do more efficiently and easily. For example, grant writing is often difficult for board members because they don't do the day-to-day work of the organization. Board members can help build relationships, go to meetings with staff, and write support letters, but staff members usually write, compile, and send the grant materials.

Provide Leadership on Policies and Staff

There needs to be clear roles regarding staff supervision.

The board hires, evaluates, and fires (if needed) the Executive Director. The evaluation process for the director needs to be done on an annual basis, and all personnel issues should be handled in closed session. Closed session means that no other staff can be in the room and no minutes are recorded as

to the specific content of the meeting. Once the board has completed a written and clear evaluation, the director should meet with the board committee (or full board if small) to receive feedback.

Evaluation is very important. The director wants to feel valued, to get some feedback, and to identify training needs, mentoring, and support.

The board should also be very clear with the director regarding expectations and work performance. If the director is not doing his/her job, find someone else quickly making use of the appropriate process.

It is the director's responsibility to deal with supervision and personnel issues of all other staff. The board should only be called upon to address any serious issue a staff has raised against the director. If the board tries to supervise other staff members, it undermines the director's authority.

The director also sets boundaries on staff involvement with the board. In some organizations, only the director is permitted to interact with the board members. Other organizations invite all staff to work independently with the board. Having other staff work closely with board members can be helpful as long as members are very careful to respect the director's leadership and authority.

The board is responsible for making sure there are adequate personnel policies for staff. The board can ask the staff to draft the policies, review them, and approve them for adoption. But the board should take the lead in guaranteeing that there are strong policies and procedures for all the organization's employees.

Legal Compliance

The board and Executive Director have a joint responsibility to ensure that the organization is legally sound.

It is part of the director's job to ensure that all of the government tax, incorporation, charitable solicitation, and other appropriate forms are filed with state and federal agencies correctly and on time. The board should review the audit and 990-tax form before it is filed to make sure the information is accurate. The staff is charged with keeping strong files that include forms and any correspondence with the government related to these forms.

The board should also regularly review the bylaws and make sure they are being followed or should check if they need updating. Lawyers and judges rely heavily on bylaws and the minutes of board meeting when legal issues are involved.

The examples given earlier for legal compliance (charitable activities, ethical money management, no conflict of interest) should also be closely monitored by the board. The staff should consistently report to the board on financial activities, any program activities that might be questioned, and any potential conflict of interest. The most common challenge in this area is to record lobbying activities and well within range of what is allowed by a 501-c-3 organization.

One small nonprofit was recently challenged on its lobbying activities. A member of the county commission was upset with the group's efforts to pass a wage theft ordinance in their community. He filed an ethics complaint with the state ethics commission alleging that the organization did not have a paid lobbyist and yet marked a small amount of lobbying on its 990 tax form.

It was a harrowing day for the Executive Director to receive a call from the state's attorney general's office for this claim. Luckily, the organization was able to justify the expenses it had listed as lobbying on its 990 form and explain why the amount was insignificant and did not justify a paid lobbyist. Currently, the attorney general is drafting a report to be sent to the ethics commission, and the organization hopes it will not hear from the attorney general again.

The county commissioner did not file this ethics complaint out of a transparent desire to make sure all nonprofits in his county are run ethically. He was angry that the organization was advocating for something he didn't want. So he tried to stop their work by giving them a scare and making lots of administrative work for their staff.

The Board of Directors must see the filings made by the organization. And the staff must record lobbying hours and keep complete files that document any activities that might be challenged by another party, no matter for what reason.

Represent the Organization

Both the staff and board can and should represent the organization in the public arena.

Often in small organizations, the staff carries the burden of media interviews, press releases, and writing. But board members are the leadership of the organization and should be organized by staff to speak and write on the organization's behalf. Staff should train board members and provide talking points if needed for a coordinated and professional communications strategy. Diverse voices will reach diverse communities and get the message out to larger numbers of people.

Other things will likely come up where it is not clear who is in charge and responsible for that area of work. The board should affirm its responsibilities and then note in its board expectations document that "All authority not reserved by the Board of Directors for itself is delegated to the staff."

Many internal problems within the organization come from confusion around board and staff roles. Here are a few tips on dealing with board and staff problems:

- Always assume good intent between all individuals working out the problems. It's good to assume that everyone is in the room because they love and care about the organization, and that everyone wants to fix the problems.

- Whenever there is a leadership transition, prioritize building relationships with the staff and/or board. If there is a change in board leadership, schedule a full board or executive committee retreat and some regular meeting time with the Executive Director. If there is a new Executive Director, communicate one on one with all the board members to build relationships as soon as possible and hold regular meetings with the board chair.

- Recruit board and staff who are willing to do work, and do it well together. Board members should think about how their work makes the staff's lives easier. Staff members should provide board members with the tools and resources they need to be leaders and make big picture decisions. If board members or staff are not doing their work, you need to find someone who will.

- Be very clear on expectations and responsibilities. Board members should have received information during their orientation about the organization's expectations and the board's role in leading the organization. Executive Directors should have up-to-date job descriptions and annual evaluations. When it is clear who is doing what, it is much easier to work together.

Chapter 3: Expectations of Board Members

The biggest complaint from board members and staff members on board involvement is that "no one told them they had to do this." Usually, this issue comes up the first time that the request to raise money for the organization occurs.

For that reason, have explicit expectations of board members and materials that outline clear tasks that board members can perform in order to accomplish those expectations. These materials should be presented to folks before they join the board, so that everyone is clear as to what is being asked.

> Board members are the governing body of your organization; but especially in small groups, board members provide a lot of support in all aspects of the organization.

The following provides an example of a job description given to potential board members to outline roles and expectations:

SERVING ON THE BOARD OF DIRECTORS

All board members have been recruited to the board because they are:
- Committed to the organization and its issues.
- Well connected to people from diverse communities and able to engage them in the work.
- Cooperative and able to work well with others.
- Willing to work to accomplish the goals.

Each board member is asked to:
1) Prepare for and attend board meetings.
   - Board meetings are held the second Tuesday of every month from 7 to 9 pm at the organization's offices.
2) Serve on one Board Committee.
   - Committees may communicate by e-mail, phone, or in-person gatherings between meetings.
3) Involve individuals and institutions in the work of the organization.
   - Identify people from your community to be involved in the organization.
   - Share names to add to the mailing list.
   - Find out about gatherings where someone from the organization could make a presentation or lead a workshop.
   - Promote educational publications.
4) Raise funds for the organization.
   - Identify funds for which the organization could apply.
   - Advocate personally for contributions to the organization.
   - Make a personally significant contribution.
5) Represent the issues and the organization to the general public.
   - Speak to groups about issues and the organization.
   - Speak to the media.

The role of the Executive Director and other staff leadership is to provide concrete goals for board members to meet these expectations and engage in the work. Many organizations provide an annual worksheet to board members at the end of the year to outline their personal commitments to the organization for the following year. Your organization's worksheet could include:

BOARD COMMITMENT AGREEMENT

1) Prepare for and attend board meetings.
   - ☐ I will attend _____ board meetings.
2) Serve on one Board Committee.
   - ☐ I wish to be on the _____ Committee.
3) Involve contacts and institutions in the work of the organization. I will:
   - ☐ Identify people from my community to be involved in the organization.
   - ☐ Share names to add to the mailing list.
   - ☐ Find out about gatherings where someone from the organization could make a presentation or lead a workshop
   - ☐ Promote educational publications
4) Raise funds for the organization. I will:
   - ☐ Make a personally significant annual gift of $_____
   - ☐ Pay for organization-related expenses, such as travel to meetings
   - ☐ Contact my contacts (foundations, corporations, law firms) on behalf of the organization
   - ☐ Add notes to letters

☐ Arrange one face-to-face meeting with a prospective donor

☐ Add five names to the mailing list

☐ Host a grassroots fundraising event

5) Represent the organization to the general public. I can be called upon to:

☐ Speak to the media

☐ Give presentations or workshops to groups about the issues and the organization

☐ Connect the organization to specific publications

☐ Write an op-ed article or blog for my local media

6) Other ways to help. I can also help with the following:

_____

For these documents to be effective, make sure all board members complete them and that everyone does what they say they are going to do. Staff or board leaders might consider doing a one-on-one check-in on board members who are behind in meeting their obligations sometime midyear.

These simple tools will provide transparency and clarity on the role of the board in leading, as well as ensure that all board members are contributing in the best ways they can to build and strengthen the organization.

Chapter 4: Role of the Executive Director to Help the Board Function

The Executive Director, as the head of the organization, has an important role in building leadership of the board and helping it function. Key concepts that guide Executive Directors in their work include the following:

Be careful of who is recruited to your board. The personality dynamics of the board can be very helpful or, conversely, very harmful. One or two difficult people can make the board completely stop functioning and dissolve the whole organization into drama requiring lots of work and energy to fix.

> So, outside of the clear expectations developed for all board members, be sure to look for board members who work well together in a group, are nice, and lead with integrity and responsibility. Don't recruit people whom you worry will cause problems.

At the same time, the director should not stack the board with his or her friends. One needs strong independent board members who are not afraid of raising tough issues.

Organize the board to focus on things you want them to do. Among the Executive Director's important roles are to recruit board members, help develop the agenda for the board, and prioritize things that need board assistance to further the work of the organization. If the director doesn't make the effort to identify what the board should be working on, the board will perhaps focus on activities that you don't want them to work on. Be clear as to what you need help with and provide real questions for board members to examine and make decisions as needed.

Plan meetings so that board members are informed and inspired. Every board meeting should include some meaty discussions and decision-making opportunities, as well as a few good stories or examples of the organization's work and impact on the overall community. Talking about the programmatic work also gives other staff members the opportunity to talk about their projects and build relationships and rapport with board members.

One nonprofit leader once served on a board for a nonprofit she loved dearly. She was willing to give up large amounts of her time and arrange fundraisers to support the organization. But she ultimately left the board because the board was unorganized and meetings were inefficient, and she felt she was wasting her time.

Ensure that the board evaluates you, every year. New boards, and especially boards with founding Executive Directors, are reluctant to evaluate directors. Nevertheless, personnel issues related to the Executive Director are a core board responsibility and the board should do its job. This is helpful not only to the director, as she gets support, feedback, and help in her evaluation, but also to developing a structure in case problems arise in the future. Don't wait for a crisis to develop a structure in addressing personnel issues (it will go badly). It's much better to have the structure in place and to address issues when they come up.

The director should encourage the board to develop a process and structure around annual evaluation, and organize board officers to lead the process if they are not currently doing so. The board should meet in closed session for the evaluation, invite the director in for feedback, and conclude with a written report that can be kept in the director's personnel file.

Provide positive feedback on board contributions. Directors should regularly tell the board and others outside of the organization that they have a great board. Why? Well, all directors want it to be true, and saying it will help make it so. This is an area where a positive attitude and strong relationships can help foster a strong board. Thank your board for their contributions. Provide clarity on where you need help. Applaud their victories!

If board members are not doing what directors need, that is a problem for the staff and board leadership to address, rather than simply putting the blame on the board.

Chapter 5: Composition and Structure

There is much variation in board composition and structure. Your organization's leadership and mission values will influence your board structure, as will the makeup of your community.

First, look at your state's requirements on board governance and structure.[1] There is some variation in state laws on what is required of directors and guidelines for organization's bylaws.

But generally speaking, make your board structure as simple and general as possible. It will take a lot of time and energy to keep up with something complicated. Also, changing your bylaws all the time is a pain, so give yourself some room to grow and change as needed before making any structural changes.

An example for a new worker rights center board could include a range of 8 to 20 board members and four officers, including president, vice-president (the person who will be president next), treasurer, and secretary.

In this example, folks might want to include in the bylaws conditions of board service such as 50 percent of the board being from the low-wage worker community, or requiring board members to live within the community. You can certainly do those things if you wish without putting them in the bylaws right away, but especially at the beginning, try not to structure the organization too much.

Do Executive Directors serve on the board? All kinds of models exist. Some directors are not on the board at all, others serve but don't have a vote, and still others serve and do have a vote. It is better to have people outside of the organization leading the work, so be careful about how your director participates on the board. The director is already a core leader (especially if she is the founder) in the organization and generally has great influence over the board's operations and functions, so further involvement in the board shouldn't be necessary.

You will also want to make sure that your board structure dictates what kind of organization you are building – that is, make sure that your form follows function. Try to structure your board similarly to the staff so that it is easy to work together in smaller groups. See that your key constituencies are involved in all levels of leadership and that the voices included are those that are most impacted by your work.

Build a board that is as inclusive as possible. Anyone who starts coming to leadership meetings has potential. Think about what kind of board leadership makes sense and constantly recruit people to fill those roles. However, don't put people on the board whom you believe will not make real contributions to the work or those who are mean-spirited and/or high maintenance.

Finally, don't take on a larger board than you can effectively work with. A very small staff will have a hard time managing a large board, which can lead to unhappy board members.

Membership

Most states have laws that dictate the minimum number of people who need to be on incorporated nonprofit boards. The number is usually three.

In the bylaws, give a range that is not too big or too small. You want enough people to

---

1. *www.harborcompliance.com/information/nonprofit-governance-by-state.php*

share work and still be able to make decisions if some of them go on vacation. On the other hand, a very large board can be unwieldy and create a lot of work to keep everyone engaged all the time. A number of people want to help but don't want to serve on the board. There are "sprinter" helpers, and "marathon runner" helpers, so think about short-term ways that others can be involved.

A helpful exercise is to look at your constituency and think about the number of people it would take to adequately represent that constituency. Also, look at the skills needed to help with the above-mentioned board roles and responsibilities.

Some organizations have both a regular board and an advisory board. If you have a lot of excellent people involved in the work but even so feel that the board is getting too big to handle, consider a two-tiered system with a smaller governing board and a larger advisory board. Some advisory boards are focused on program work, fundraising, or outreach in the community. Sometimes it's also easier to recruit for an advisory board because usually less of a time commitment is involved. An advisory board can be a very helpful group of supporters, if members have a clear purpose and are consistently tapped in ways that strengthen the organization.

> Who do you want on your board? For many community-based and social justice organizations, it is important to have diverse voices from the community providing leadership on the board. This often includes those who are most helped or impacted by your organization's work.

Be thoughtful about who is asked to be on your board. Last year, IWJ hosted a training session for worker center leaders who were mostly low-wage workers. One woman was so impressive in her questions and comprehension of budget issues that staff asked her in between sessions what other type of nonprofit board experience she had. She said she had never served on a board, but certainly knew how to budget because she never had enough money in her personal life!

You want folks from the community on your board who will be leaders (people who can bring in other people), with skills that will help build the organization. You want people who are kind, caring, and smart. You want people that will work. It should never be a token representation. Having a vacant spot on the board is better than having someone there who isn't going to help.

Board members should also have skills that are needed within the organization. An accountant could help review the audit, a board member with access to wealthy people could help with fundraising, and an HR person could help with personnel issues. Board members who work on recruitment should understand what the skill needs are and think about what kind of board member might fill them.

Terms

Board members need to know about terms. A term is the length of time the board member is asked to serve. You should have term limits that are not too long and not too short. There are quite a few groups with board members who have been serving for more than 20 years! A hard-working board member should be tired after serving on your board (asking their friends for money, volunteering, doing media, making policy, growing the organization, after all, are quite time consuming and sometimes stressful), and you should let them put their energy into other things. Or they can put their energy into your organization in a different way such as advisory boards or committee work.

The bylaws should explain board term limits as well as how unexpected vacancies will be filled owing to death, resignation, or removal due to nonperformance of duties.

Terms also allow you a friendly way to get rid of people who are not fulfilling their commitments as board members. Make your terms long enough that you have consistent leadership and are able to move the work forward.

The most common terms are two or three years per term. Each board member can serve no more than three or four consecutive terms before having to leave the board. And then the board member has to take one or two years off the board before being considered for service again.

Make sure you stagger your board classes. One new director inherited a board in which members served a three-year term and could only serve two terms at a time. Unfortunately for her, she quickly realized that the board had not been enforcing this policy, nor had it been staggering board classes. She set up staggered classes, but now every year (for the next three years) one-third of her board has to retire and she is stressed out by having to recruit, train, and engage that many new board members every year.

Here's an example illustrating a staggered class board:

Interfaith Worker Justice of New Jersey
2013 Board membership currently 12 members (can have 10–20 members). Terms are three years and members can serve up to three consecutive terms for a total service of nine years.
Officers:
President: Becky Waller
Vice-President: June Anderson
Secretary: John Cade
Treasurer: Lucy McDonald

2011	2012	2013
John Cade (1)	Becky Waller (3)	Derrick Horton (2)
June Anderson (2)	Lucy McDonald (1)	Katrina Brogie (2)
Megan Schroeder (3)	Adam Allende (1)	Joe Burkett (3)
	Erik Davis (1)	Sofia Gutierrez (1)
	Don Romero (1)	

The number next to each name indicates which term the person is in. This is a fairly new board, with lots of potential for growth and support of the organization.

Since the current number is only 12, the board may decide to continue to recruit new members to get closer to the 20-person maximum. But to keep the number at 12, the following recruitment would be necessary:

2014 – one new member; ask John Cade and June Anderson to renew their terms

2015 – one new member; ask Lucy, Adam, Erik and Don to renew

2016 – one new member; ask Derrick, Katrina, Sofia to renew

For consistency in leadership and planning, tiered president and vice-president office positions are a good idea. All officer positions can be three-year terms. The vice-president is the person who will succeed the president, so this office involves a longer commitment: three years as vice-president and three years as president.

Quorum

Quorum is the number of voting board members you need in the room in order to make decisions. Many states have requirements on what the quorum should be, but usually it's the majority of board members. When setting the quorum, don't have it so low that a small number of board members have the power to make big decisions. But if it's too high, it could be difficult to get things voted on and completed, so issues could drag out over time. At least half of the voting members plus one is good practice.

Committee Structure

Depending on the board size and staff size, a committee structure can help focus and drive board members' efforts to lead the organization. Consider the following committees:

- Executive Committee. This committee consists of the officers, typically the president, vice-president, secretary, and treasurer. The president chairs the committee. This committee often serves as a personnel committee (to evaluate the Executive Director and address any grievances against the director) and as a smaller collective advisor to the Executive Director.

- Finance Committee. This committee is made up of the money folks. The treasurer chairs this committee. This committee reviews the audit and 990 tax form, examines financial reports closely, and recommends/helps develop financial policies as needed.

- Fundraising Committee. This committee is composed of the raising money folks. It can be chaired by an at-large member with fundraising experience. This committee approves the fundraising plan, engages the board in fundraising, and manages any grassroots fundraising efforts in which the board has leadership. Sometimes this committee is merged with the Finance Committee in case the board is small, since the income and expenses are so intertwined.

- Board Development Committee. This committee recruits, develops, supports, and, if necessary, fires board members.

It can be chaired by anyone on the board with interest or experience. This committee should accept recommendations from staff and board on potential board members, review candidates, invite members, provide board orientation and support, and propose removal of members as needed. This committee should also track the board classes, and lead board self-evaluation processes.

- Program Committees. Depending on your mission, additional program committees could provide important support to your board. Some examples include organizing (for issues and campaigns), communications (focused on outreach, marketing, and social media), and public policy (for education and advocacy on policy issues).

Each board member picks a committee, but be sure that everyone picks one that connects with his/her skills and experience. Sometimes you might gently nudge new board members into committees that really need the help.

Don't create more committees than you have staff and board members for. If there are only five board members, it's not easy to have five committees. Some functions can be combined if necessary. The idea is to provide smaller groupings for folks to strategize and take ownership over a manageable part of the work. The two committees the board must have at all times are the Executive Committee and Finance Committee.

Finally, don't over structure yourself in the bylaws. You can say that the "Board will form committees as needed to accomplish the mission of the organization." That provides flexibility for the board to modify itself over time without having to go back to the bylaws.

Chapter 6: Meetings

Most people don't like meetings, so it is your organization's responsibility to make sure board meetings are easy to schedule, engaging and productive, with follow-up steps so that work can get done between meetings.

Meetings also provide an opportunity to build and strengthen relationships among board members. A cohesive and positive board will be a more effective board.

Scheduling/Preparing for the Board Meeting

The number of meetings you have depends on the type of work you do and how the board is involved in that work. Most boards with a community-based focus meet monthly or bimonthly.

> Be sure to plan out your meetings a year at a time and make the time consistent (like the third Monday of every month, from 7 to 9 pm, at the organization's offices).

Send out information to board members a week before the meeting to remind them about the meeting and provide an agenda and preparatory materials to review beforehand. The e-mail to the board members can include:

- Reminder of the date, time, and place of the next board meeting

- Minutes from the last board meeting (for those who weren't there or need reminding about what happened)

- Meeting agenda

- Handouts needed to review in advance

- Reminders of what board members should think about in advance of the meeting. For example, if the primary agenda item is to review and vote on providing a retirement plan for staff, board members should be instructed to review the three different options and think about the discussion questions staff has provided in order to make a decision.

Try to send all the information in one e-mail so that no one will get confused about what was sent, or feel overwhelmed by the number of e-mails received with pieces of the meeting.

If you only hand out materials or present new projects without materials at a meeting, those who need a few days to reflect beforehand will be at a disadvantage and won't participate as fully as possible. Many people need materials and proposals ahead of time in order to report thoughtfully.

Turnout is very important, so ask your board members to confirm whether they will or will not be attending the meeting. And call or e-mail folks you haven't heard from so that you have a sense of the attendance.

Also, always have a few hard copies available for those who forget their paperwork. Some board members will just use their computer or tablet to access the information, but others will want paper copies and not have their own.

Running an Effective Meeting

Board meetings can be effective, productive (and even fun!) gatherings of the organization's leadership. A number of things can be done to make sure everyone is in the right frame of mind for an effective meeting.

Set the stage by following good party rules. Start the meeting on time and end on time. One board member served on a board with meetings scheduled from 7 pm to 9 pm, but sometimes the meetings would keep going until midnight or later. Needless to say, the board member didn't stay on the board very long! Make sure the room is comfortable for everyone – the lighting should be good, the temperature should not be too hot or cold, and the chairs need to be sturdy and comfortable enough for a couple of hours of sitting. You might also provide food and drink or ask board members to switch off bringing treats to share.

Focus the meeting on decision-making. Board members should be addressing the most important issues facing the organization, discussing and grappling with real questions, and making decisions. The staff needs to prepare all the information that will allow the board to make good decisions, or the staff should delegate appropriate decisions to the executive committee. The types of agenda items include budgetary matters and launching a new program – any topic that falls within the board's responsibility.

The agenda should be varied and should address what is important and needs to be shared. Thus, not every committee or person needs to give a report at every meeting – except the financial reports, of course! The financial report should be reviewed and discussed at every meeting. The committee reports and other leadership reports should be presented in the context of the meeting's main discussion. If there are other committee reports to be shared, they can be included in the mail to the board to be reviewed.

Board members should never be surprised by organizational crises, so make sure the board meeting agenda reflects matters that are most important to the organization and tries to address issues in the early stages before they become bigger problems.

Make sure the meeting is led and run by the board. Many organizations rely on the Executive Director for everything, so that the board meeting becomes a report by the director and does not engage the whole governing body. It takes work to prepare board members for their roles in the meeting, but it promotes ownership and leadership within the organization.

The president or chair of the board should approve the agenda and moderate the meeting. The treasurer should provide the financial report. The secretary should take the minutes, send them out to all members promptly after the meeting, and keep a copy on file with the organization. These minutes should include all decisions made in motions and votes during the meeting. Other board members should be prepared to report on agenda items where they are working in a leadership capacity.

> During the meeting itself, everyone should try to engage as many board members as possible. Certainly the chair can help facilitate this, but everyone should help make sure all voices are heard and that there is time for questions before making decisions.

Make sure there are clear next steps and that leaders have assignments to be completed before the next meeting. The last ten minutes or so of the meeting should be spent clarifying what needs to be done next and who will do the work. This keeps the momentum going and sets forth responsibility and accountability among the board members.

Minutes and Follow-up

The board secretary (or staff doing the draft with secretary approval) should type up the meeting's minutes, including next steps and important future dates for the organization, and send them promptly to board members after the meeting.

A copy of the minutes with appropriate attachments should also be kept with the organization for its historical records. Recording minutes is considered a best practice of nonprofit operations, and folks like your auditor, the government on Form 990, and groups like the Better Business Bureau will ask if you have copies of the minutes.

Finally, the board should survey itself about the effectiveness of meetings once every couple of years. As board members change, new leadership might want to do things differently or incorporate board training or educational presentations into the occasional agenda.

Chapter 7: Strengthening Your Board

Creating a wonderful board takes time and energy. This chapter suggests some best practices on how to strengthen your board to be the best it can be.

Orient All New Board Members

When a new member joins the board, provide a strong orientation for the person to understand the organization, its structure, finances, and role and responsibility of the board in leading the organization.

The orientation itself only needs to take an hour, and ideally it is handled by the Executive Director and board chair with all the new board members together.

A board orientation manual provides the structure for the orientation session and additional reading materials. The following materials can be included in an orientation manual:

Organizational History and Current Goals and Objectives
- History
- Mission and Vision
- By-Laws
- Articles of Incorporation
- Strategic Plan
- Annual Goals and Objectives

Board and Staff Information
- Board of Directors List
- Board Classes
- Job Description
- Staff List with Primary Responsibilities

Financial Information
- Annual Budget
- Fundraising Plan
- Last Year's Audit Report or Letter of Financial Review

Recent Board Meeting Minutes
- Minutes from the Last Six Months of Meetings

Ask the Board to Evaluate Itself

The Board of Directors should also evaluate itself every two years to reflect on the body's effectiveness, strengths, weaknesses, and priorities moving forward.

No board is perfect, and it's nearly impossible to address every issue. The goal of the assessment is not to make anyone feel bad about everything the board should be doing, but rather to see if there are any big gaps in the board's work that needs to be addressed and how to promote growth by prioritizing some new work for the next year or two, until the next evaluation.

There are many tools online for board self-assessment, some of which are pretty complicated.

It would be valuable to spend a couple of hours answering some basic questions, working in small groups to discuss everyone's answers, and coming back together as a larger group for reporting back, seeking agreements on next steps, and planning to make the board even better than before.

Basic questions might be to rank the primary responsibilities of the board 0–5 or N/A (with 0 as bad and 5 as excellent):

- Set program priorities.
- Maintain financial integrity.
- Provide leadership on policies and staff.
- Ensure legal compliance.
- Represent the organization.

Provide an opportunity for folks to talk about the effectiveness of how the board is formed and structured:

- Composition and structure
- Meetings (especially asking how they can be improved)
- Membership
- Communication between board and staff

Set board development goals to make the board even better:

- Board member recruitment
- Training needs
- Fundraising

This is a good activity for a board retreat to celebrate the successes and good work of the board as well as to identify some areas of work and incorporate that work into the overall agenda for the leadership.

Build Community on the Board

Because relationships are so important to getting work done, to function more effectively and efficiently the board needs to build a strong sense of community. Encourage an annual board retreat or ongoing opportunities for board members to bond and learn more about each other than just their common interest as being a part of the organization.

Give Your Board Meaningful Things to Do

Board members have skills and experience that can help build the organization, but they often need to be told what they can do to help. The board should develop and approve clear board member job descriptions (expectations) for members and officers. Every board member should be asked to complete an annual worksheet outlining the specific ways they will help the organization as a board member.

It is the director's responsibility to know

every board member and invest in the relationship to ensure that every board member is doing meaningful work.

Also, the board should have an easy way to communicate with each other and should be kept abreast of any major happenings in the organization. Most boards have distribution e-mail lists or have set up a Google group as a way of sharing information. Essentially, if you are on the board, you should find out about things before other folks do.

Recruit Strong Leaders

Incorporating new board members with distinct skills and expertise can improve the effectiveness and capacity of your organization. But who are you looking for to serve? And what skills do they need?

> Do a board self-assessment and create a board profile. What skills and expertise does the board currently have? What skills do the board and organization need? Who are some possible candidates who meet that skill set?

It is important to recruit folks who are close to the issue and represent the community, but also make sure that these persons have the skills to contribute to the board in meaningful ways.

Next, create a nominating committee of the board that recruits new members. This committee develops a recruiting process and is responsible for presenting potential candidates to the board, reaching out to recruit new members, and orienting new board members.

Everyone on the board should think about appropriate people to serve on the board. Consider inviting long-time volunteers. Volunteers dedicate consistent hours and understand the work of the organization. They can often be terrific additions to the board. Also think about board members who are retiring from leadership in other organizations. Have a conversation with the staff of other organizations to see if there are board members who can build bridges between organizations, and think, too, about trading retiring board members (with their permission!) to strengthen relationships.

Who **has a conflict of interest** and shouldn't be on your board:

It can be difficult to find board members. As one director said, "It's not like board members are knocking down my door." Nonetheless, do not put the following people on the board:

- Married or partnered couples. They could vote together and influence each other in organizational matters.

- The spouse or partner of a staff person. Although it is admirable that someone's partner shares the same values and passions as the staff person, there are other ways to coordinate that type of work. Again, the potential conflict of interest between staff and board is a big deal.

- Staff members other than the Executive Director. One founder of an organization shared the news that he had hired two people who were sitting on the board, but then no one asked them to leave once they became employees. There are two problems here. First, the director will be evaluated by two of his employees, whom he also supervises. Second, board members cannot provide adequate oversight if they also serve on the staff.

Having these people on your board is not against the law, but why open your organization up to ethical or conflict of interest questions by your enemies and make yourself more vulnerable? Recruiting and developing new leadership should be a core strategy of any growing nonprofit, so it is worth the effort to find other members of the community to serve on the board.

Leadership also needs to be developed from those currently sitting on the board. Observe and nurture potential leaders by providing opportunities to be involved and connected with other board members with experience and wisdom. Encourage those who have energy to lead committees and be officers.

Invest in Training

Much like staff, board members don't always come into leadership with all the skills and experience needed. This can be a good thing, as it provides an opportunity to incorporate training into building board leadership.

Provide regular continuing education opportunities for board members, either occasionally during board meetings or during a planning retreat. This could be skill-building training (such as how to read financial reports or conduct a legislative action), introduce a new program, or learn more in-depth information about a current program.

Planning retreats encourages relationship building, strategizing, and training for board members. Many boards do a full-day session once a year or an overnight session once every couple of years at an off-site, special location. The agenda usually focuses on some big picture thinking such as developing a strategic plan, creating a process for Executive Director transitions, or doing a self-evaluation. But including a training component can also break up the day a bit and give members time to reflect on their work or learn about something new.

Finally, board members should have an easy way to communicate with each other in order not only to keep board members apprised of the organization's activities, but also to foster learning among members. Often staff and other members can share information about a relevant training to attend or events related to the work that might be of interest to the leadership.

Conclusion

The Board of Directors should be a core piece of your nonprofit organization. It is well worth the time, effort, training, and systems to develop a strong board. A strong board will reflect the values of your organization, honor your mission, and provide trust to your donors that resources are spent with integrity.

Section 3

Office Systems and Management

Introduction

1. Databases

2. Insurance

3. Office Supplies and Furniture

4. Files Management

5. Getting Special Help from Experts

6. Interns and Volunteers

7. Other Organizational Policies

Introduction – Order, Efficiency, Practicality

Office systems should make your life easier and support your core mission. Operations should be organized in a way that is practical and works for the organization and its programing. Smart office management is keeping an orderly office that requires as little time as possible. This chapter gets into the nitty gritty of operations, focusing on the areas where hard lessons have been learned by many an Executive Director.

For example, one organization lost a grant because when the new director came in, the filing systems were inferior and she had missed the grant renewal deadline. The lost grant meant an even tighter budget, which was a big stressor during her first year. Another director allowed the bookkeeper to keep the books open at the end of the year. When a new director was hired and figured this out, big mistakes were found that board members didn't know about.

Please read on so that your organization won't make the same mistakes!

Chapter 1: Databases

"It is a capital mistake to theorize before one has data." – Sherlock Holmes

A database is an important tool for keeping track of volunteers, donors, members, and others. Databases enable organizers to keep abreast of many of these relationships and to keep in regular contact with as many people as possible. For instance, you might know all the core members and supporters of your organization, but if you were asked to get together the phone numbers of all the people who have come to one of your group's events in the past three years, how long would it take you? If volunteers come in for a few hours, can you quickly and easily show them how to print out all the mailing labels so they can put together a mailing on their own, or do you have to spend an hour pulling together an address list from several different sources? Do people who have expressed interest in or attended your group's events ever get lost in the shuffle? How well do you keep track of financial gifts (including gifts by individuals) so you can follow up appropriately? Do you have the kind of quantitative information that funders often want for grants?

The sooner you create and begin building a decent database, the better off you will be. The only way to grow is to have systems that allow you to grow. It does no good to contact greater numbers of people to build support for your group if you do not have the capability to maintain effective contact with them. As a result, your organization can accomplish more if you think intentionally about your database use.

What NOT to Do in Developing a Database

Almost every nonprofit has made a number of mistakes in database creation and maintenance. Technology changes quickly; no one has much money, and people have even less time. Here are some of the most common problems:

Developing a Database for the Short Term. Sometimes, the database that is fastest in the short term will hurt you in the long term. If the director and sole staff-person of a group is working on a campaign, for instance, that person often keeps track of participant contact information by simply creating an Excel spreadsheet with all the people involved in that campaign. This approach may work while you are dealing with that set of people for events related to that campaign, but if the group wants to call those people a year later for a different event or if you want to pull together all the people who have been involved in different campaigns for an organization-wide event, it becomes more complicated. It may also work while you only have 50 to 100 names because you can copy and paste 100 people's addresses into a Microsoft Word label form without too much trouble, but when you get up to 200, 500, or 1,000 names, you want a system that can easily export the right information you need so that labels can be made more easily.

A new nonprofit started using Excel to track donations. Volunteers entered the gifts and sent out thank you letters (irregularly, but that's another story). In less than a year, the organization received close to 1,200 gifts from individuals, religious organizations, foundations, and corporations. The Executive Director realized a better system was needed for tracking gifts, and gave a volunteer the assignment to start moving the records from Excel to the new database. The volunteer started the project, and early on accidentally moved the gift amount column away from the names of the donors so that the gifts were no longer correct for each person. She saved the document with her work and *no one noticed the mistake for three weeks*. By then the previous version of the document could not be found and retrieved. During this time period, no one received donor thank you letters.

Luckily for the organization, the director had hardcopy records of all of the deposited checks. But then a new volunteer had to go through each check and reenter the information into a database. It took weeks and the organization couldn't send a mailing it had planned for its one-year anniversary newsletter and appeal for support. The mistake cost the organization time, money, and headaches!

Building Different Databases for Different People. A new development director of a growing and exciting immigrant rights nonprofit revealed that his staff's biggest project was not raising new money, but getting the organization's many "databases" (Excel spreadsheets) integrated in one place. They had spreadsheets for individuals who came to events, donors, media contacts, workers, individuals who gave e-mail addresses – probably six or seven spreadsheets in all. They had QuickBooks (an accounting software program) records for donor contributions, and staff had individual e-mails in their work e-mail accounts. They also did

not have a spreadsheet for any donors who attended events in the last five years and paid cash for their tickets.

The development director had already tasked two volunteers with starting to integrate the system, but thought it would take them at least a year to get everything organized – a year before he could strategically start to do his job!

What a mess. Why do we need different databases for different people? Donors should be invited to events. Workers should receive direct-mail appeals. Media contacts should get the e-newsletter. Any good database program should have ways to identify the different ways a person is involved with your organization, integrate that information, and provide reports that you can use for communications, fundraising, and getting involved in your work.

An exception to this rule would be when there are issues of client confidentiality. This could be those receiving legal advice or private information.

Overdoing the "Do-It-Yourself" Mentality. Every nonprofit is trying to do a lot with limited resources, so sometimes staff try to create databases themselves rather than seeking software that can make things easier. This approach may be "penny-wise, pound-foolish" because the resulting database often takes an enormous amount of the staff-person's time to create and then may not be designed to serve all of the organization's needs or to grow with the organization.

So, buy it. Over the last five years, databases have gotten so much better, easier, and cheaper for nonprofits. Some programs are free up to a certain number of records.

It may also pay to use an expert to migrate your data into a database, to ensure that it gets set up correctly and that a knowledgeable expert can identify problem areas before they are institutionalized in a new system.

What To Do to Build an Effective Database

Talk through the Process with Somebody Knowledgeable. If you know database software or you have a good sense of computer technology and know-how to figure out new programs, you may be able to buy a program and then personalize the database yourself. At the very least, though, talk through the process with somebody (perhaps a friend of your organization) who knows database technology and the needs of your organization. You can also reach out to the Nonprofit Technology Network (NTEN) in your area at *www.nten.org*. NTEN offers free workshops and local tech meet-up groups where you can learn from other nonprofit tech professionals. Idealware is another good resource at *www.idealware.org*, which has lots of articles and reports on different software.

Make sure you do it right. This may sound obvious, but on numerous occasions, groups have created databases that did not work properly, and they ended up spending much more time and energy to fix the problem than it would have taken to simply do it right the first time.

Think about How You Want to Be Able to Communicate with People and make sure your database supports that kind of communication. If you have two hours to make turnout calls for a rally or a volunteer comes in for half a day, how do you want to be able to sort your lists so you can target those calls most effectively? Sometimes, it helps to be able to sort people geographically, so you can only call those in the neighborhood of your action, the neighborhood of the workplace in question, the congressional district of the representative you are targeting, and so on. Other times, you may want to sort people on the basis of your organization's campaigns in which they have been actively involved.

Here are some general functions your database should be able to perform:

- Organize and sort basic contact information.
- Generate lists of phone numbers, physical and e-mail addresses.
- Track the events people have attended.
- Track the gifts people have given.
- Track the number of people involved in various campaigns and events.

Each database is set up differently and has a number of standard fields that everyone needs (name, address, e-mail, phone number, fax). Fields are the heart of a database program, so put some thought into additional fields you will need ahead of time such as:

- Salutation (Dear _____) so your database can record whether you address the person formally, for example, Mr. or Ms. "Last Name", or informally by first name
- Title (Mr./Ms./Rev./etc.)
- Suffix (e.g., Jr.)
- Organization
- Type of organization (e.g., congregation, union, denomination, etc.)
- Web site
- Professional title
- Address type (home or business)
- Congressional district
- City council or other local political district

- E-mail

- Twitter handle

- Facebook name

- Source of the name – which member of your organization established contact with the person?

- A "do not send mail" box to check if people do not want to receive your mailings

- A "do not send e-mail" box to check if people do not want to receive e-newsletters or solicitations

- Assistant/secretary name

- Assistant/secretary phone

- Assistant/secretary e-mail

- Events the person has attended (and dates)

- Contacts the organization has made to the person

- Gifts the person has made (and dates)

- Other ways the person has been involved in the organization (board member, volunteer, intern)

- Additional Notes – dated comments from staff and leaders who have been in contact with the person

- Anonymous Donor Status – for those who do not want donations to be made public

Any other fields you think might be useful

Think about Integrating/Syncing/Automating as Much as Possible. Many groups contract with different companies for databases, accounting software, e-mail programs, Website hosting, and credit card processing. You want to find programs that are in sync with and that share information with one another and are automated or integrated as much as possible.

For example, Interfaith Worker Justice used to have four different databases or lists: donor management, e-mail and online advocacy, credit card payments, and name collection from the Website. Staff members used to export names from the database to the e-mail program every time they wanted to send an e-mail. Then, if new e-mail addresses were captured by the Website, they had to be manually entered to be included on the mailing list. Sometimes it took a couple months for new people to receive mail from the organization. Also, if someone made a credit card gift on the Website or through the mail, it had to be manually processed through a third party company, separately deposited through the bank, and manually entered in the accounting software. What a waste of staff time! IWJ now has a synced database that accounts for e-mail (no more exporting and manually syncing) and a credit card processor that automatically processes the gifts from its Website and then deposits those gifts, minus fees, into its bank account.

Aside from the staff and volunteer time involved, the greatest value of an integrated database is that it gives the organization a bigger picture and understanding of the people involved in the work. Staff can see patterns of when someone gives and what causes people care about they can also tailor communications and work to build stronger connections and grow relationships with those people. Opportunities are missed if there's no analysis on what works and doesn't work with constituents.

Buy a Database Program. There are so many good cheap programs out there that are designed for the particular needs of nonprofits that it makes good organizational sense to buy a database program. In order to do that well, you will need to have at least a basic sense of what kind of database you want and the kind of budget you have. Be careful to set a budget that includes any setup or maintenance fees, and is affordable in tight budget years. The most important thing is that you use the simplest program that is capable of doing what the organization needs done. Extra complications just get in the way and make the database harder to use. At the same time, think about how many names you have now but also how many names you want to have in the next few years so that you can construct a database capable of growing with the organization. If you have a number of staff who travel or work from home, a Web-based system is crucial. If you don't, then go for a cheaper, simpler non-Web-based system that can be easily networked in the office.

Getting a new database can seem a daunting task. Don't do it alone. The person/people in your office who will use the database the most (even those who are the least computer savvy) should have a big say in which program is chosen. Everyone should be able to use it. A few tips on buying software:

- *Don't hurry.* You might need time to budget adequately. Don't just include initial cost but estimate ongoing tech support and staff time to launch and update the database. Also talk to your staff and volunteers about how they use data in the organization. This is a big decision that can be hard and time consuming to fix later.

- *Do your research.* These two guides, produced by TechSoup and Idealware, are excellent places to see and compare some programs. They will give you a sense of what you are looking for and need from a database program.

  - *http://www.techsoup.org/support/articles-and-how-tos/do-you-need-a-new-donor-management-system*

  - Consumers Guide to Donor Management Systems *http://www.idealware.org/reports/consumers-guide-donor-management-systems*

Also, talk to your friends who work for other nonprofits and see what they use. A colleague recently went to a conference and asked several allied organizations about their software, and was surprised by the number using the same program. It resulted in a helpful conversation about why that program was chosen and some of the challenges in using it for their purposes. Many in the small nonprofit world are using Salsa Labs, GiftWorks, CivicRM, PowerBase, DonorPerfect, and Salesforce.

- *Play with demos.* Most database programs allow you to try a sample version of their program for free. Reach out to the company and ask for a demo. It is a very helpful way to spend a couple of hours, especially for organizations that aren't clear about what they want/need. Invite computer-savvy staff, volunteers, or board members to participate and ask questions. It is often much easier to see what is needed once you get to see and test actual programs with your data.

- *Negotiate the price.* This is a highly competitive market to get your business, so don't be afraid to ask for discounts, waiving some initial fees, or getting a few licenses for free. If you are in a position to sign a contract for multiple years, you should ask for serious discounts. If you are exploring two companies at the same time, it can be a very good way to compare apples to apples and get a better deal. Be very careful to understand the length of the contract, penalties for getting out of the contract, and tiers for future pricing for licenses or number of records. Think about the future and growth and the ongoing expense of any program you choose.

The best product for you might not always be the cheapest product. Be willing to spend money on the functions you really need. It will save you lots of staff time, and thus money, in the future.

Database Maintenance and Other Things to Consider

Maintaining the Database

Every person who contacts your organization, attends an event, or is referred as a potential contact, should be entered into the database. It is useless to create a database unless you are going to update it regularly. If you have the right kind of volunteers, you may want to give this task to them. Since entering contact information correctly is extremely important, groups should give this task to volunteers only if they are well-trained, detail-oriented, somewhat computer savvy, and willing to work regularly with the database. There is a learning curve. People entering data for the first time will always make some mistakes, so it's important to find folks who will learn the system correctly and enter information accurately. If you do not have regular volunteers, it makes more sense to enter data yourself than to give it to people who are volunteering on a one-time basis.

Managing and maintaining the database should be assigned to one staff member who will be in charge. In one small nonprofit, an organizer was reassigned half of her time to work managing the data. It is important to have clear lines of responsibility and accountability on who is in charge. Whoever that person is should also have the authority (or access to the authority) to get other staff to complete their responsibilities and use of the database.

You should have a simple organizational strategy on building and maintaining your database. Start small. Could you set a goal to increase the number of e-mails you have by 10 percent by the end of the year? This is so important for growth and for creating institutional memory among those involved in your work. At least once a year, staff, board, volunteers, and leaders should be asked to add names to the organization's database. It should be part of your culture for staff to continually collect and add names to build the organization.

Also, every 1 to 2 years you should get your data cleaned. Duplicate records, old e-mail addresses and mailing addresses can quickly make a database irrelevant and costly to repair. There are mail houses that provide this service through the U.S. Postal Service (their National Change of Address service) or database companies that can often provide it for additional cost.

Finally, make sure you have as many e-mail addresses of people in your database as possible. Engaging people through technology is cheap, quick, and efficient. It is important for quick mobilizing around issues and urgent fundraising requests. If you have lots of names and mailing addresses without e-mails, there are services you can purchase to find their e-mails. It's usually a cost per e-mail found, which doesn't have to be too expensive if you do some at a time, especially for those active in your organization. Then you can send them an e-mail request to join your e-mail list and receive information electronically.

Security

Since you are putting a great deal of personal information into a very easy-to-access format, security is an important consideration. Depending on the database program, two easy options include putting a password on the computer that houses the database so that only authorized users can log onto the computer, or putting a password in the database program so that only authorized users can use the database specifically. If you are worried that people who do not know how to use the database will accidentally mess up your data (which is very possible!), you can also allow only certain users to change or delete data and limit other users to searching your data without the ability to change or delete.

Database Resources

Idealware, *www.idealware.org* – Idealware helps nonprofits implement smart software solutions. There is an abundance of reports and articles on this site.

NTEN, *www.nten.org* – The Nonprofit Technology Network is a membership organiza-tion of nonprofit technology professionals who want to help nonprofits use technology more effectively. There are some very helpful articles and free webinars on its site.

Progressive Technology Project, *www.pro-gressivetech.org* – The Progressive Technology Project is a progressive organization and foundation that provides training and technical assistance on technology use for social change organizations. They also run Power-Base, a database built for organizing.

TechSoup, *www.techsoup.org* – This website contains resources on nonprofits and technology. Also, if your organization registers with TechSoup, you can buy lots of different software at deeply discounted rates. IWJ buys almost all of its software from TechSoup, and it has saved the organization thousands of dollars.

Chapter 2: Insurance

Having the proper insurance policies is a must for the sustainability of any nonprofit organization. It is crucial to protect the staff and leadership through good benefit policies like health care, disability, and workers' compensation insurance. At the same time, you need insurance to protect programs and activities from financial or legal problems that could ruin the organization. Before purchasing any insurance policy, consult with a good broker or attorney and do a needs assessment for the different types of insurance you might need. It shouldn't cost anything for a broker to ask you some questions and make recommendations on what insurance would protect your organization best. The most common types of insurance policies held by nonprofits are listed below.

General Liability

This is the core insurance policy for a nonprofit organization, sometimes called "slips and trips" insurance. It protects your organization from liability in the case of things like:

- Bodily injury (someone is injured on your property, or you cause an injury on someone else's property while working)

- Damage to your property (like fire, flood, theft)

- Personal injury (such as libel or slander)

Insurance companies often offer property insurance, but you don't need that if your stuff isn't too valuable. Just make sure you know how much your property, equipment, and supplies are worth and that your insurance covers the amount it would cost to replace it all.

When looking for this insurance, make sure you are covering the above situations. You also want to look for a policy that al-lows annual changes: As your organization's programs change, you may need to adjust the amount of your coverage or add some different types of coverage to your policy.

Finally, look for an "occurrence" policy, not a "claims made" policy. An "occurrence" policy provides coverage for claims made when the policy was in force, but regardless of when a claim was reported with the insurance company. However, a "claims made" policy only provides protection for claims that arise and are reported when the policy is in force. If a claim is reported after your policy has expired, your organization will not be covered by the policy, even if the incident happened when you had insurance. An occurrence policy will provide much better and long-term protection for your organization.

Directors and Officers

This insurance policy is designed to protect both your nonprofit organization and your Board of Directors against lawsuits brought in cases involving employment-related issues, discrimination, and sexual harassment. More than 75 percent of claims filed against nonprofits and 90 percent of Directors and Officers (D & O) claims are employment-related (negligent hiring or supervision, wrongful discharge, discriminatory practices, and related grievances).

When looking for a D & O policy, make sure that you can cover your organization's board members, staff, volunteers, and the organization itself. Also consider the activities of your organization and decide whether your activities are risky enough to warrant buying D & O insurance. The premiums for this policy can be quite expensive, although in some cases it can be sold as a "rider" to your general liability policy.

Despite the cost, many nonprofits purchase D & O because it supports a strong Board/staff relationship and can improve the governance of the organization. If the Board and staff are assured that they are protected from lawsuits and personal liability, they may be more likely to serve and lead the organization in a strong and powerful way. Also, some potential board members won't join a board unless there is this type of coverage, and you don't want to miss out on good leadership!

Shopping around for Insurance

The insurance business is very competitive for nonprofit organizations, so it's important to shop around before purchasing any insurance policy. As is true of other types of specialty fields, a broker is well worth the money. Find an expert who works with other nonprofit clients like yours, who is fairly easy to reach, and who you like working with.

A new staff person was trying to figure out if her organization still had an active general liability and D&O insurance. She was having a hard time reaching the broker; he would only respond to her if she contacted the insurance company directly and they called him.

She worried that her organization didn't have coverage and was upset that her broker wasn't helping her. Advice for her? FIRE the broker! She was trying to both work with what she inherited from others (bad broker) and be nice by continuing to call him. Nonprofits, regardless of size, should be valued and important clients. If the broker isn't working out, better to find someone who will work than wasting time with an ineffective person.

A good broker should be able to take the relevant information for your organization and tell you what coverage you need, how much coverage you should get, obtain different quotes for that coverage, and provide

ongoing support for any questions or issues that arise relating to the insurance policy and coverage. The broker is paid by the companies themselves, so it's folded into the price of the policies.

Before you meet with a broker, there is some basic information you should collect to make sure the meeting is as efficient is possible:

- Know your North American Industry Classification Code (NAICS), formerly the SIC code. Your NAICS code affects the companies that will provide quotes for your organization. It's not clear how the codes are assigned – some by the Census Bureau and other government agencies[1] – and for that reason are a pain to change. Ask your broker if the NAICS code is affecting your quotes and if it is, work together to try and get it changed.

- Get a rough idea of what your organization owns (computer, office equipment, translation, etc.) and how much it would cost to replace it. This information will be helpful in determining what kind of insurance you need.

- Find out what other types of insurance your work may require. Do you have employees using their own cars for business? Then ask your broker about nonowned/hired auto liability coverage. Attorneys will need malpractice insurance. Ask your broker what other nonprofits have in your area and why. Sometimes it is worth getting quotes on additional coverage, even if you don't end up buying it, just to know how much it costs and to weigh the advantages or disadvantages of spending the money.

Then, during the meeting with the broker be sure to ask about the amount of coverage

---

1. *www.census.gov/eos/www/naics/faqs/faqs.html*

your organization needs. For small nonprofits, a total $1 million in coverage should be enough, but make sure your broker makes a recommendation after looking at your history, program work, and types of coverage you need.

Your broker should also provide a quote that bundles any possible products together. Like many things, you can get a discount if you buy more products from the same company. The key to this issue is to find a company that you like and trust, so it's easy to want them to hold more of your business.

Once your insurance needs are met, educate your board on the costs and coverage of the insurance your organization provides. One new nonprofit director asked her board about directors and officers insurance and wanted to know why the board had decided not to get this coverage for the organization. The board, consisting of attorneys, did not know they did not have D&O coverage! The situation was quickly fixed, but as the board has liability if something bad happens, it is an important reminder to keep them informed about the organization's coverage.

An overwhelming amount of information on different types of insurance can be found at the Nonprofit Risk Management Center (*www.nonprofitrisk.org*), a nonprofit research and education center regarding insurance and risk management issues for community-serving organizations.

Chapter 3: Office Supplies and Furniture

Every nonprofit organization with an office needs basic supplies and furniture to function. However, many of these items can be quite expensive, and not many organizations have a lot of resources for fancy desks, state-of-the-art copiers, or even cushy toilet paper!

There are deals to be had on supplies, furniture, and technology; you just need to know where to look. This section should help you get started.

Office Supplies

One office manager in a small nonprofit organization estimates she spent 10 hours of her workweek last year going to four different office supply stores to get the best deal on paper, folders, and computer toner. However, the cost of her staff time looking for these supplies was likely greater than any cost savings the organization thought it had.

Convenience, price, and quality play important roles in ordering office supplies. For that reason, the best option on buying office supplies is to determine which office supply companies (Staples, OfficeMax, Quill, Costco) service your area and set up a business account with that store. The cost tends to be lower, you can keep a history of your orders so it's easy to reorder when needed, and most items come the next day. Items are easily paid for with a credit card, which is a nice way to pay if your nonprofit has a card with points or miles.

For the first order, be sure to price shop for the most common supplies needed and comparison shop between them. Then stick with a company for a while and see if you are happy with its service and products.

A few nonprofit networks offer discounted office supplies through companies as a part of membership, which could be a useful discount. There's also one company in California, Give Something Back Office Supplies, which gives a percentage of its profit on supply sales to nonprofit organizations. These value-added companies are increasingly popping up, and using them could be a more socially responsible way to buy supplies.

There are also a few Websites that provide corporate donations to nonprofit groups, with the groups paying some for shipping. Two of them are Good360 and NAEIR.org (this group requires a membership fee). The products of these Websites change all the time, but the Websites have bulk products like post-it notes, bulk crayons, paper products, and cleaning supplies.

Finally, think about asking folks in your community for help. Keep an ongoing wish list on your website for donors to give (some people like to give things over money). It's always surprising to see who might have a scanner or small refrigerator sitting in their basement to donate. Check with your local city council member's office to see if there are any green products like CFL light bulbs that might be free to nonprofits, like CFL light bulbs.

Furniture

New office furniture that is of decent quality is expensive! But there are several ways to get quality pieces that last and look nice and professional.

- *Craigslist*. This Website is a treasure trove for all kinds of things, including office furniture such as desks, lamps, chairs, and file cabinets. Be sure to check out the free board to get things, well, for free. You will need to pick up, but a truck rental and some muscle could be well worth it.

- *Free Cycle.* Many communities have strong free-cycle groups that post things needed or wanted and give them away for free. Again, you will need to pick up.

- *Commercial recycling office furniture company.* Depending on your community, there might be a company or nonprofit that recycles office furniture. There are many in California and New York where you can set up a wish list of what your organization needs, and browse through a catalog to claim free office furniture.

- *Allied organizations.* Get cast-offs from allies that have more money than you do. Often banks, law firms, unions, and universities upgrade their offices and don't have need for that conference room table, file cabinet, or chair. You can help them out by picking them up and giving a tax-deductible letter for an in-kind contribution.

Other Things You Might Get Cheaply

Software. If you are a 501-c-3 organization, you may qualify for deeply discounted software through TechSoup, *www.techsoup.org*.

Computers. Small-business discounts are available through almost every major company. If you use one particular type of computer (Mac, Dell), approach that company directly and see what small-business discounts might be had. Or try a company, like CDW, that sells technology to businesses directly.

Incorporating Your Organization's Values into What You Buy and Use

Supplies and equipment are two major areas where your organization is a consumer and where your values can be reflected in what you buy and use. Here are a few thoughts on values you might incorporate and how to do it:

Frugality
Being frugal reflects a value of responsible stewardship of your resources. Folks will use less if you set up easy ways for them to do so. So:

- Keep office supplies in one place and encourage everyone to put their extras there and use up all supplies before buying new ones.

- Put a box by every printer with one-side printed paper so that it can be used again for printing.

- Buy only what you know you will need.

- Use everything up before buying something new (except for stationary and other things that will take awhile to get reprinted and are cheaper to print in bulk).

Conscious about the environment
Offices use a lot of stuff and generate a lot of waste.

- Make sure your office has a recycling program that incorporates as many materials as possible.

- Buy thrift store mugs, plates, and silverware so everyone can share and not use up plastic/disposable paper goods.

- Purchase a water pitcher for shared filter water.

- Buy as many recycled products as possible. Office paper, paper towels, toilet paper, and plates can all be purchased recycled.

Worker-friendly

Do your research to find free trade coffee; union-made computers, shipping services, and cell phone plans; socially conscious companies; and local distributors that give back to your community. Don't use your organizational dollars on companies that exploit others.

Healthy and safe environment

You show respect and caring for your employees when you provide them with equipment that encourages a healthy and safe office. That means you might have to buy a new office chair, ergonomic keyboard, or air filter for those who need them.

Professional workplace

Just because you ask for and receive donated materials doesn't mean that your office has to look junky. Don't accept pieces that don't make sense for your office or are going to give it a cluttered appearance. Take the time (and if necessary, spend the money) to remove old things from your office on a regular basis and keep things organized. Also, if the money is available, focus on what will make your staff do a better job. A faster computer, a smartphone for staff who travel, and a printer that is quick are all things that add to the professional appearance you seek and that those on staff seek when representing the organization.

Chapter 4: File Management

Managing the files and keeping files accessible is important to nonprofits for a number of reasons. The biggest is that a number of documents are required by law to be kept as long as the organization is in operation. But other reasons include developing an organization's institutional memory and history, and not reinventing the wheel for things that have been done in the past.

Unorganized files can also be incredibly stressful for staff. Several years ago, there was a small social justice organization that had a one-room office donated by a law firm. The director was overwhelmed by all of the different hats she was required to wear as director, and one source of her stress was messy files. She inherited a full file cabinet of stuff she didn't know what to do with, so she just bought some banker boxes and started putting her own stuff inside. Every time she needed a grant report done, she spent hours looking for any file that might have had the original proposal. She finally started taking the time to organize her files and found a whole bunch of stuff she's been able to use since. It was well worth her time.

There are a number of things you should absolutely keep. The reasons you keep something should be at least one of the following:

- It is the law to keep it (there are a bunch of files that are permanent records).

- It is a core part of your organization's history.

- You will need it in order to do your work better/easier/faster.

When developing a file system, think organizationally. If you have files that don't make sense to anyone but you, but are needed by the organization, you need to think about a new system. Anyone in the organization should be able to understand how the files are organized and be able to find what is needed without additional help.

The following list presents the basics that you should have in place. For many of these, just add the new information to the folder once it changes:

- Administration
  - Articles of Incorporation
  - Bylaws
  - 501-c-3 Tax Letter
  - Other Organizational Policies
  - Sales Tax Exemption Letter

- Administration – Board of Directors
  - Board of Directors Lists
  - Meeting Minutes
  - Finance Committee Meeting Minutes

- Administration – Staff
  - Personnel Policies
  - Personnel Files of Current and Past Staff
  - Payroll Records

- Communications
  - Newsletters
  - Organizational Brochures, Annual Reports, Outreach Materials
  - Special Event Materials, Project Materials
  - Photos, Marketing Materials

- Finances
  - Audits
  - 990 Tax Forms
  - Budgets

- Fundraising
  - Foundation and Corporation Folders (labeled with Foundation name, in alpha order)

○ Major Donor Folders (labeled with donor name, in alpha order)
○ Fundraising Appeals (by year)
○ Fundraising Event or Sponsorship Materials
○ Annual Fundraising Plans
○ Direct Mail Appeals and Coordinating Response Cards

- Program Work
○ Conferences/Training/Events
○ Outreach Materials
○ Policy Campaigns

Of course, there may be additional files depending on your organization's mission and work. But these will provide a solid base of institutional history as well as keep some things in order that will need to be found to continue to do good work.

Electronic Files

Increasingly, there are even more electronic files than hard copy files for small nonprofits. Documents can be easily downloaded from a Website or e-mailed, and lots of folks use laptops and tablets for meetings, so not as much needs to be printed.

However, electronic files should still be organized and kept for accessibility and history. These types of files can be searched by title or topic, which makes it more likely you will find what you are looking for. Also, for documents like grant applications, it's helpful to have some drafted material to copy and paste from when writing several applications to raise money for one program.

Organizing electronic files is much like organizing hard-copy files. Files that are final documents should be organized as such and kept in a way that's accessible and transferable to other folks in the organization. The above structure (Administration, Communications,

Fundraising) would also work for organizing electronic documents.

The individual can keep any draft documents or things that are still being worked on until the document is completed. Then it should be moved to the "organizational" folder related to the topic.

If your organization has one computer, keep your organizational records on that computer. It must be connected to an external hard drive (which you can easily buy) and backed up every day. If you travel with this computer, the external hard drive stays in the office. If the computer is always in the office, take the hard drive home or place it in the care of someone in a leadership position.

If your organization has more than one computer, get the computers networked and set up a shared drive through which folks can leave their work and put final documents in the appropriate folder. Newer computers have networking capabilities, and the Internet has a lot of material on how to set up a small-business computer network. Or, of course, you can find an expert to do it for you. Your network should have a way to back up its data every day on an external hard drive. It should be taken home with someone on staff after a data backup is completed so that no data is lost.

One caution on shared drives is that you will have less privacy. Be aware that other colleagues could access your files, change them, or delete them. If you have sensitive information on a shared drive, be sure to protect the file so that information stays private.

Finally, just like the hardcopy files, electronic files get messy and occasionally need organizing and cleaning. Staff should make sure that any organizational documents get moved to the right folder, that former staff documents are organized or deleted, and that the document retention/shredding policy is being enforced so that any appropriate material is deleted.

E-mail

Electronic mail is an often-overlooked part of files management. Yet most who work in an office write hundreds of e-mails every week about work and attach important files to that correspondence. It also constitutes a written record and history of your organization.

E-mail is overlooked because every person has an individual account, and the data tends not to take up very much space on a server or computer memory. But ALL of that data is owned by the organization and can be requested in legal cases.

So be sure to have guidelines for staff on e-mail. They can be included in a document retention policy and include the following:

- Staff will use Auto Archive (if using Microsoft Outlook) to delete old e-mails automatically.

- Staff will not store or transfer work-related e-mail on nonwork-related computers except as necessary.

- Staff will take care not to send confidential information to outside sources.

- All old, archived e-mails will be permanently deleted from the server once a year.

Document Retention/Shredding Policy

In most offices, there are groups of people who don't want to get rid of anything and those who want to get rid of everything!

When it comes to files, a more moderate approach is required that saves the documents that are necessary but gets rid of excess copies, individual files that don't contribute to institutional memory, and an organization system that provides storage for things that are important.

A document retention policy is a good way to keep all of this organized. This policy used to be called a shredding policy, but electronic documents and e-mails provide valuable information and should be included.

You can find many examples of document retention policies online. Yours should have the following components:

- *Purpose.* Necessary records and documents of the organization must be adequately protected and maintained and records that are no longer needed or are of no value need to be discarded at the proper time. It also helps employees and volunteers understand their responsibility for hard copy files, electronic documents and e-mail.

- *Suspension of file disposal.* When the organization is informed about any audit or legal matter regarding its documents, it must stop disposing of any documents until the Executive Director, with advice from counsel, deems otherwise.

- *Staff Responsibility.* What does the staff have to do to abide by this policy? Clean out documents once a year? Keep institutional files on the shared server? Any expectation related to staff on this policy should be in this section.

- *Types of Documents.* A number of documents should be kept permanently. Others can be kept for any period defined as reasonable by the organization's board. Time periods are suggested below.
  General Correspondence
  ○ Records on routine matters should be discarded within two years.

- Records with significantly lasting consequences or for archival purposes should be retained permanently.
- Records relating to a particular project or campaign should be kept for the same period as the project is current and active. Once the project is completed, most documents related to that issue should be discarded within two years. The only exception is those documents that contain historical value for the organization, which should be given to the Executive Director to be kept separately for that use in the future.

Electronic Documents
- E-mail. See above for suggestions regarding the policy for e-mails.
- Electronic Documents. Guidelines are the same as hard copy documents.
- Data Back-up Plan.

Contribution and Grant Records
- Records of contributions are permanent.
- Other grant records such as grant proposals, grant agreements, grantee financial and narrative reports kept at least 7 years after the completion of the grant period.

Accounting and Finance
- General Ledger, Journal Entries, Audits, Budgets, and Cash Receipt Books are permanent.
- Bank statements, financial statements, employee travel reports, expense bills, and credit card records should be kept for at least 4 years.

Contracts
- Vendor contracts and agreements and leases (after conclusion) should be kept for 7 to 10 years.

- Corporate Records such as incorporation papers, minutes of board meetings, annual reports, bylaws, IRS letters, licenses, and permits are permanent.

Payroll Documents
- Employment history, employee records, timesheet recording spreadsheets, payroll register, and group insurance reports are permanent.
- W-2s, payroll tax returns, unclaimed wages, and timesheets should be kept for at least 3 years.

Pension Documents
- Documents are permanent.

Many nonprofit organizations have confidential or sensitive documents in their possession. The question that should be asked when reviewing such documents is whether these documents would be damaging to an individual, your organization, or another organization if they fell into the wrong hands. If the answer is yes, you should keep the documents (hard copy, electronic, or e-mail) only for as long as necessary and then get rid of them. It is not uncommon for large corporations or other bodies to subpoena nonprofits for documents or sue them directly. Be careful about what you keep in case someone looks for it later.

Archiving

While you are getting files organized, consider your organization's place in broader history. Do you have things related to your work that someone might want to see in the future? Do you get e-mails from students asking to write about your organization and/or work? Do you think that the work being done now will have made a contribution to a wider movement in the future?

If so, consider deliberately saving documents, educational materials, photos, and videos that might be of interest to someone in the future. You can certainly do it internally (i.e., keep a file called "Archive" electronically and hard copy for this purpose), or you could seek out a professional archive to organize, store, and protect your organization's documents. An archive would also offer your documents to the public for research and writing. The only downside to an archive is that the documents given to them become their property, so you would be unable to take any of the materials back.

Here's a great resource on what groups should keep it is called *Don't Throw it Away!* University of Illinois at Chicago University Library: *www.uic.edu/depts/lib/specialcoll/pdf/DTIA.pdf*

To find an archive, look at the colleges and universities in your area and find out which ones have special collections of materials like yours. Many archives have particular interests and will let you know if your organization's records might be a good fit for their collection. Do your homework and meet with archivists and visit their collections. Archives are not all the same, so pick one where you have a good relationship and can trust that your organization's documents will be safe, yet open for those who want to learn more about your historical work.

Chapter 5: Getting Special Help from Experts

It is impossible for nonprofit staff and board members to know how to do everything in running a nonprofit. Every person is given a set of skills, gifts, and experiences and uses them to the best of his or her ability. Sometimes it is better to get help and not try to be trained in everything.

The president of the United States is very aware of this dynamic. President Obama expressed a desire to focus his decision-making on issues of importance to the country, and so he decided to forgo making certain mundane choices. For example, he only wears the same type of gray or blue suit, and he doesn't think about what he eats for lunch.

In nonprofit operations, there is so much detail in every area of work, and it can be incredibly frustrating and daunting. In small organizations, leaders don't have time to be experts in everything. And the work can't always be perfect.

But that doesn't mean anyone should settle for bad work and chaos. Hiring or getting experts can be a tremendous help to operations work. Here are the big areas a professional is worth seeking:

Information Technology (IT)

There is a smart, committed nonprofit director who is most insecure about her technology skills. She feels that her organization would be stronger/bigger/better if she were stronger on technology.

Her low-tech office was really struggling. The staff was still using Microsoft Office 2003, and she said it was starting to impact their work. In that year PowerPoint was not given as part of the suite, so anyone who needed to develop a presentation had to go home to

work. But most seriously, no one could read a file with a. docx extension, which is most commonly used by those with 2010 software and newer. The outdated software was becoming a real problem and was embarrassing for staff.

Why didn't they upgrade? The software was cheap to buy through TechSoup,[2] but she was terrified that she would be the person who had to install it all. What if issues arose that she couldn't fix, or what if files got lost? IT consultants, even cheap ones, were paid at least $50 an hour, and she didn't have that cost in the budget. She finally found an IT volunteer who was willing to help her, but this solution was a few years in the making.

This director should not need to know how to install and troubleshoot software problems. The lesson for her was that she should have found someone, volunteer or hire, a long time ago and should have made it an administrative priority.

IT consultants do so much to help streamline your back office. Formatting computers, installing software, setting up a shared drive, backing up your data, maintaining your server – the list goes on and on. Are there areas where office technology is getting in your way of doing good work? Then you should call on an expert to get it right. There are many IT folks willing to volunteer for a good cause, and a number of consultants who charge modest rates to nonprofits, even contracting a monthly flat rate for basic services. If you are in a building with other nonprofits, consider getting a shared contract with one consultant to save some money.

---

2. *www.techsoup.org.* A great nonprofit that sells software and other tech tools to other nonprofits for a deeply discounted rate.

Websites

It is crucially important for your organization to have a Website where you can communicate your message to donors and members, show photos/images of your work and its impact, have a space to make a donation, and provide contact information. The Website needs to be updated regularly.

Having such a site should not require you to have coding skills or to build something from scratch from Word Press. Yet it's not an easy thing to develop something that is pleasing to the eye, simple to use, and has basic functions like being able to make an online gift or download an educational document directly from the Website.

If you have a Webpage-savvy staff-person, it's worth adjusting his/her workload so that the person can manage the Website. If that alternative is not feasible, then hire a design firm, advertise for a volunteer Website designer, or find an IT intern from an area college or university. The key to finding someone is to make it a defined project with a modest scope. You are more likely to find someone willing to help for a month or two to revamp your organization's Website than if you were to look for someone to become an ongoing webmaster responsible for the Website forever.

Graphic Design

Marketing is extremely important for fundraising and outreach for your organization. Groups often think that lots of money should be spent on full-color brochures with glossy paper and tear-off pages. Of course that would be nice, but money and time are better spent finding someone to design your core outreach materials and Website. The design makes a huge difference in a person's perception of your work and willingness to get involved.

There are graphic design firms who do some *pro bono* work, students who are looking for practical experience, and volunteers who care about helping nonprofits.

Think about what materials would be best served by having them professionally designed and would last for a while like your Website, organizational brochure, or flier for a program or training that happens regularly. Make sure to ask if the material can be designed in such a way that you can make simple edits (like changing the date to the event) in a software program you already have, and is formatted in a way that can be printed by any office printer. Also be clear about whether the design can be used for anything else. Maybe the designer does a poster, but you want to use the same color scheme and border for a flier or stationery. Make sure terms regarding ownership are clear so that no one gets upset.

Data Clean-Up and Enhancement

No one has perfectly clean data. It gets messy with growth and age and so needs a good tune-up every once in awhile. The big things that happen in databases are duplication of records, old addresses when someone moves, and change of e-mail address. It is important to have volunteers who will keep up with your data as much as possible, such as changing addresses when mail is returned or responding to e-mail requests to be added, removed, or changed on your list. But it can be expensive to mail to a bunch of inaccurate addresses, so every couple of years have your mail house or database company clean up your data.

Data clean-up time is also good because it makes database entry a priority for a while. Encourage your board to get those new addresses in before the clean-up happens, or ask staff to go through their contacts list and e-mail accounts, making any changes needed before the information is sent out for cleaning.

Data enhancement is another way to improve your data. If you need phone numbers, e-mails, or addresses for your records, it could be worth paying a service to get this information. In newer organizations, often records are just name and e-mail so the person might not get a newsletter or direct mail appeal. In older organizations, it's often the opposite, with records that have names and addresses and not e-mails. The goal depends on how you communicate with your base, but generally e-mails, letters, and phone calls are all ways that organizations want to communicate with their base.

Payroll Service

If you have a decent amount of changes in your payroll processing, or feel nervous about being responsible for the payroll and tax reporting for your organization, a payroll service can help. The service is responsible for processing all of your employees' paychecks, making sure the appropriate state and federal taxes are withheld, paid, and reported, making any deductions for retirement, transportation, or health care for each employee, and distributing their W-2s. Many groups use an accounting software program's (like Quick-Books) payroll module, but it's often just for salaried employees with the same amount processed each time. If you have hourly employees with changing hours or even if payroll just takes a lot of staff time, a service can help a lot. ADP, Paychex, and Paycorp are three companies that work a lot with nonprofits. Make sure you are comfortable with their services and bargain on the price!

Bookkeeping

Many nonprofit staff members are not comfortable around money issues, and that especially includes the bookkeeping. Most software programs are easy enough to use, but most staff don't have much understanding of nonprofit fund accounting, and the kind of information to put into the system for good financial reporting. A number of retirees and people who have small bookkeeping companies work with nonprofits. Could this be a place to combine hours with another nonprofit in your building for a better rate? A volunteer could do this for you, but you would need to make sure the person was very trustworthy and willing to do it on an ongoing basis. Be very cautious about using a volunteer to do your books. Having tight control on the money is most important.

Legal Services

Legal letters and phone calls from lawyers can be very challenging for nonprofit leaders. The letters are always so official looking on paper, written in dry language that's hard to understand. The best way to assuage fears is to find your own attorney to help navigate the legal process. Lawyers often are required to do a certain amount of pro bono time a year, and so many of them seek out opportunities to help local nonprofits. So reach out to law firms, bar foundations, law schools, or public interest clinics in the type of law that you need to seek help.

And be sure to keep good files on anything legal. Copies of final documents sent and correspondence received should be kept both electronic and hardcopy files. Make sure your organization has its own copy of everything sent on your behalf.

Finding Pro Bono Services

A few places to look for pro bono services include the following:

- *Taproot Foundation.* This organization provides in-kind grants in a whole range of areas, including marketing, database, and human resources. Your organization has to be headquartered in and around Chicago, Los Angeles, New York, San Francisco Bay Area, or Washington, DC, in order to qualify. The quality of help is very high, and while it's competitive, it's a very helpful and comprehensive program that provides some much needed help.

- *Bar foundations, law schools, and law firms.* These resources in your area offer legal assistance. IWJ has always found pro bono help for any legal issue that has arisen, ranging from a subpoena requesting documents to a question about employee benefits. There are many good and passionate attorneys out there, so you just need to make friends with your local lawyers and ask for their help!

- *Student consulting groups.* Specific classes in both undergraduate and graduate schools are looking for ways to help nonprofits and provide a service to the community. Some degree programs worth looking into include business, social work, nonprofit management, peace studies, and specific classes that may relate to your organization's work.

- *Other businesses.* Most corporations like to tout the amount of pro bono work they do every year to support the community. All you need to do is build a relationship with them so they can support you! Ask a grocery store for donations for your fundraiser picnic, or an accounting firm for a free/discounted audit. Website builders, graphic designers, IT folks, PR and marketing firms – anyone who is in business for profit likely has some service to give back to the community. It's definitely worth asking. The worst they can do is say no!

Paid Experts

If your organization is using a paid consultant or contractor, be sure to have a written contract. The contract should indicate services required, amount that will be paid, deadlines, and any other key information related to the project. For example, include ownership of the project deliverables in any graphic design or other media contract. The contract should be signed by both parties, and a current version should be kept on file.

Chapter 6: Interns and Volunteers

An important way to involve people in your organization's work and build your capacity to do more of that work is to get interns and volunteers to help. Giving work experience to interns especially also develops learning and leadership in young people who will help build the next generation of nonprofit leaders.

Finding Unpaid Volunteers and Volunteer Interns

Finding reliable volunteers, and then managing them effectively, can be a very challenging task. Everyone needs volunteers and acknowledges their value to the organization, yet volunteers usually need a significant amount of supervision and support.

The best volunteers are those already involved in the organization as donors, newsletter subscribers, or attendees to an event. Many volunteers have heard a staff-person speak publicly about the work and want to help out. Or if you have a big single project, you can partner with local volunteer service organizations to help.

Consider looking for volunteers in the following places:

- *University job/internship fairs.* It's a great place to meet college student interns and potential volunteers.

- *Schools.* IWJ has had volunteer interns from masters in social work programs, seminaries, and even a school of psychology! Local undergraduate and graduate institutions often have community service requirements for programs, clinical practice programs, or classes with service components.

- *When you are out speaking.* Make sure to connect with folks after a presentation or workshop and talk about volunteer opportunities.

- *Senior centers or senior programs.* Many public countywide senior centers are on the look-out for service projects. One of the largest is the Retired and Senior Volunteer Program. RSVP volunteers are all over the country and are a great help in lots of administrative projects[3].

- *Idealist.org.* This is a large Website with nonprofit jobs and internship opportunities. You can post a job description here for unpaid intern positions.

The media have recently given extensive coverage to the legal and ethical use of unpaid interns in all types of workplaces. The Department of Labor does have guidelines for internships, but it covers only for-profit companies.[4] Some employers are starting to pay interns minimum wage in order to acknowledge their work and also to make their internships more accessible to diverse candidates.

It is not always possible to offer paid internships. In cases of unpaid programs, have a strong learning program in place so that leaders are being developed by working with you, and not just doing the jobs no one wants to do.

---

3. Find if there are RSVP volunteers in your community at *www.nationalservice.gov/impact-our-nation/state-profiles*

4. *www.dol.gov/whd/regs/compliance/whdfs71.pdf*

Finding Paid Volunteers and Interns

Small nonprofit organizations can beef up their staff by recruiting long-term paid interns or volunteers placed through community service fellowship programs lasting between ten months and two years. These programs often have great, committed and passionate folks and the cost is affordable, even for a small budget. Most of these programs require strong ongoing supervision from host organizations.

People who are interested in community service and social justice apply to these programs, and organizations apply for the opportunity to host a "volunteer." (Some volunteers receive room, board, health care, and a small stipend.) The programs then match volunteers with organizations based on the needs, skills, and interests of both parties.

The following list is not an exhaustive one, but hopefully it will give a sense of some of the programs that exist with long-term volunteers.

Long-term Volunteer Programs

Updated January, 2014

Program	Length/time commitment	Age of most participants	Annual cost	Geographical limitations	Contact info
Jesuit Volunteer Corps	1 year (August to August), full-time	21-30	$11,000-$19,000, depending on housing prices and various other costs	Depends on the region; call JVC regional office to find out	www.jesuitvolunteers.org each region has a different phone number (available on website)
Lutheran Volunteer Corps	1 year (August to late July), full-time	21-30	$10,000-$18,000, depending housing prices, the budget of your group, and various other costs	Placement sites are Baltimore, Chicago, Milwaukee, Minneapolis/St. Paul, Seattle, Tacoma, Washington, DC, Wilmington, DE, Oakland/Berkeley/ San Francisco, Omaha, Atlanta	www.lutheranvolunteercorps.org (202) 387-3222
United Methodist US-2 Program	2 years (September to August), full-time	20-30	Around $10,000 – contact the program for more information	None	http://new.gbgm-umc.org/connections/ youth/us2 or contact the General Board of Global Ministries, (212) 870-3620
United Methodist Mission Intern Program	3 years, 18-month international work/study assignment and an 18-month action/education assignment, full-time	20-30		One's own country	http://new.gbgm-umc.org/connections/ youth/interns or contact the General Board of Global Ministries, (212) 870-3620
Dominican Volunteers USA	11 months (August to June), full-time	21-30	$11,000- $19,000, depending on housing prices and various other costs	Dominican communities in the US	http://dvusa.org/volunteers/prospective/ index.html (312) 226-0919
Brethren Volunteer Service	1 year (several different start and ends points), full-time	All ages	$5,000-$7,000	None	www.brethren.org/genbd/bvs/index.htm (847) 742-5100 or (800) 323-8039
United Church of Christ Partners in Service	Flexible placement length, full-time hours	All ages	Similar to JVC, LVC, and US-2 – contact the program for more information	US only	www.ucc.org/volunteer/partners-in-service
Avodah: the Jewish Service Corps	1 year (August to August), full-time	21-26	Contact the program for more information	Placement sites are Chicago, New York, New Orleans, and Washington, D.C.	www.avodah.net (212) 545-7759; info@ avodah.net
Franciscan Volunteer Ministry	1 year (several different start and ends points), full-time	22-30	Similar to JVC, LVC, and US-2 – contact the program for more information	Placement sites are Camden, NJ, Philadelphia, PA, and Wilmington, DE	www.franciscanvolunteerministry.org (215) 427-3070
Jewish Organizing Fellowship	1 year (September to August), full-time	21-30	Contact the program for more information	Boston	www.joinforjustice.org/programs-projects/ jewish-organizing-fellowship (617) 350-9994 ext. 205 (Helen Bennett)
Mennonite Voluntary Service	1-3 years (several different start and end points), full-time	20+	Similar to JVC, LVC, and US-2 – contact the program for more information	US only	www.mennonitemission.net/Serve/MVS/ Pages/Home.aspx (866) 866-2872
Ignatian Lay Volunteer Corps	Typically ten months a year, 2 days a week	50 and over	$1,000	None, volunteer in own community	www.ilvc.org (410) 752-4686, toll free (888) 831-4686
Americorps VISTA	1 year, full-time	18+	Contact the program for more information, additional info at www.nationalservice.gov/node/12358	US only	www.nationalservice.gov/programs/ameri-corps/americorps-vista

Be careful to note the difference between asking someone to volunteer and promoting an internship. A volunteer is someone who is there primarily to help your organization for free and to do whatever needs to be done; an intern is someone who is getting a learning experience out of the work. If the intern is unpaid, be careful that the intern is not operating as a staff person. If you can't provide a learning experience or time for good supervision, look for volunteers.

Finding Work-Study Students

Although the work-study program is neither a volunteer nor a pro bono program, it is well worth your organization's time to explore getting qualified as a federal work-study site with a local university. You will need a very strong relationship and also the administrative capacity to deal with the billing and supervision of the student. This means offering work-study internship opportunities to students (but consider the note above) at no cost to the organization; but also to students looking for jobs. A work-study position can be any defined job needed by your organization that can be filled by a student – for example, administrative help, management of the Website and social media, fundraising assistant, and so on, for several hours a week during the whole school year. The school reimburses the organization through the work-study program for a good chunk of the cost. The students make $10/hour to work, and your organization pays roughly $4/hour of that expense. A great way to get some extra help! It's also great because if you find a student who is a good fit, you might have the same student for a few years while he/she is going through school.

Tips on Working with Volunteers

Volunteers can play a crucial role in the organization's ability to meet its mission. Volunteers can do everything from serving as board members to stuffing envelopes for the year-end mailing. But managing volunteers can be tricky. Here are a few tips to avoid common problems:

Create a structure for volunteer roles and expectations. If you use volunteers on a regular and ongoing basis, it is worth the time to develop a small volunteer program to manage those folks. Create job descriptions for ongoing volunteer roles, provide training to volunteers to perform those roles, and create a schedule for volunteers to follow.

Also be clear with volunteers as to expectations and things they may not do within the organization. A director of a new nonprofit organization stated that her biggest issue with volunteers is that they had all these ideas and started projects in the name of the organization that she couldn't possibly keep up with. Things started to fall apart when the volunteers didn't follow through on their commitments. She had to rein in their efforts and provide greater clarity regarding what was appropriate for volunteers to do within the organization.

Screen and fire volunteers. Don't feel like you have to accept any and all volunteers. Difficult people will cause problems throughout the organization. So ask for resumes and conduct an in-person interview before asking someone to volunteer. And if someone isn't working out, you have to fire him or her in a professional manner.

Another reason to screen volunteers is to make sure the person is trustworthy. There has been an increase in the number of attacks and thefts in nonprofit organizations, so be thoughtful about questions that will tease out the motivations and intentions of the potential volunteer.

Only take the volunteers you can handle. If you can only provide meaningful supervision for five volunteers, then don't take more than that. It takes a decent amount of staff time to organize and manage volunteers, and there will be a point where too many people, despite their good intentions, will become disorganized and do things that aren't helpful to the organization. Maybe you can take more in the future, but prioritize the work that needs to be done and take only as many as you can provide a good experience for.

Give volunteers meaningful work. Volunteers come to nonprofits because they want to contribute to society and find meaning in their own lives. If you don't give them a range of work, and work that really can help, it's hard to keep happy volunteers. So yes, give them those phone calls and data entry projects, but give them context on how those projects help the organization and mix it up with other types of work. Ask about their skills and experiences and tap them into your organization as much as possible.

Thank your volunteers for all of their work! When folks are not acknowledged for their contributions, they won't stay involved. So think of ways to thank your volunteers. A hand-written note for something extraordinary, or an annual thank-you reception for volunteers can go a long way to express your gratitude and build deeper relationships within the organization.

Keep in touch with your volunteers and interns after they leave. Most folks volunteer or intern at your organization because they share

similar passions and values as the nonprofit. Make sure all your volunteers and interns are entered into the database and that the records are kept current. Also, being able to connect with former interns who are working in your field can help in coalitions, program issues, as well as finding and recruiting new interns.

Setting Up an Internship

There are several components to consider when setting up an internship opportunity within your organization.

School Policies

Every school is different, but many schools' service learning and internship programs require that a student be supervised and mentored so that the experience will be as educational as possible. The student is not allowed to spend too much time on administrative office work such as filing and answering the phone.

The contract your student has with its school or program is the student's primary agreement. You should learn what is included in that agreement before bringing anyone new on the staff. Any policies that your organization has related to operations, discipline, or personnel can be included in the internship, but only if it is not addressed in the program agreement.

Job Description

Write a job description for the internship, but recognize that it may change depending on who fills the position. Think about how you would like to deepen and expand your organization.

Think, too, about the kinds of tasks that can be accomplished by the end of the internship. Is there a major event coming up that needs more help? Or do you need support for your organization's core programming? It is very important that students get the opportunity to build relationships with people in the community, especially those outside of their school community.

Every good job description will include:

- A purpose
- The name of the supervisor
- A clear list of responsibilities
- The percentage of time the intern is expected to spend on these responsibilities. Often there is a limit to the amount of administrative work that can be listed in the job description.

Supervision

Some interns come in with knowledge and experience, while others may require a lot of training and supervision. Ask the intern what skills he or she has and what skills he or she wants to build. Sit down with the intern at the beginning to evaluate how much and what kind of supervision he or she will need. Co-create a work plan for the length of the internship. It might need to be progressive, changing a little as an intern grows in the position. Check in with the intern at least weekly so that you can get a sense of how the intern is doing and what additional training or instruction he or she may need.

A few other questions to think about:

- How much knowledge and experience does an intern need to have in order to be useful to your organization?
- How many hours, weeks, or months will an intern need to work in order to make it worthwhile to spend the time training that person?
- How does the school's schedule fit into your organization's schedule?

Volunteers and interns are vital for nonprofits. Small organizations never have enough staff. Your challenge is to be sure to balance your need for help with your ability to effectively manage and benefit from others' work. There may be times when it feels like it's more work to train a volunteer than to do it yourself. Consider it an investment in the big picture of your work. Many volunteers and interns will be your best supporters and best advocates. Internships are also a powerful way to develop the leadership of others to join your field of work and cultivate the next generations of leaders for social change.

Chapter 7: Other Organizational Policies

How many policies do small nonprofits need, anyway? Although you might be small, your operations are not any less complicated than those of a much larger organization. So the answer is – a lot. But so much depends on the legal requirements, program activities of your work, and culture and history of the organization. It is easy to see when an organization has weathered a traumatic experience because it shows up in the policies. A five-page policy on data protection? Pages and pages about identifying sexual harassment? Something clearly has happened to cause such extensive policy-making.

Organizational policies are useful because they are written codes of conduct that can be easily followed and enforced. Policies don't have to be long and overly complicated; they can be short and sweet. Some are quite short and could easily be added as sections in your personnel policy.

Policies Needed for the 990 Form

All functioning nonprofits need to file a 990 form every year, which is the nonprofit tax form. Your income dictates the version of the form that you need to file. The smaller your organization is, the easier the form. But in 2008 the 990 form was revised to include much more information on governance, and it asks about the following policies on the form. While the IRS doesn't require you to have all the forms, it does provide suggestions for best practices, and most people wouldn't want to raise any flags for a government visit by not having these policies, so why not?

- Conflict of interest policy
- Whistle blower policy

- Document retention and destruction policy
- Expense reimbursement policy

The other two policies that might be needed are:

- *Joint Venture Policy.* If your organization is going into a formal joint venture or partnership, you need a joint venture policy.
- *Gift Acceptance Policy.* If your organization is thinking about or has been offered a nontraditional gift like a car, or boat, or building!

Other Core Policies for a Strong Nonprofit

Many of these policies can be included in your personnel policy or union contract, and are very good practices to have addressed:

- *Written code of ethics.* It's good to have a policy regarding how you expect people in the organization to operate and behave while on the job. It's helpful in developing a strong organizational culture.
- *Nondiscrimination policy.* No one wants to discriminate, so make that statement clearly. Funders often require this one.
- *Equal Opportunity Employment Statement.* This statement verifies that your organization is committed to fair employment and inclusive staff.
- *Substance Abuse Policy.* This policy sets forth a value of safe environment and a drug-free workplace. Funders also often require this.
- *Sexual Harassment Policy.* This important policy protects all employees.

- *Anti-Terrorism Policy.* This one is required by many foundations and can serve as a protection to your organization that you aren't promoting terrorism. (Sigh)

- *Health and Safety in the Workplace.* This policy promotes wellness and safety in the office.

- *Ban on nonpartisan activities.* Small non-profits have to be very clear that their employees cannot participate in or intervene in any political campaign or candidacy on work time. Employees can participate in the political process on their own time, but must publicly separate their personal activities from their professional responsibilities.

Additional Policies – Program Work, Organizational Culture, Code of Conduct

- *Dress Code Policy.* This policy involves an expectation of how your organization represents itself in public through dress. This is especially important for organizations that do a lot of public speaking or reach out to diverse audiences. IWJ calls this the "church lady policy." If you wouldn't wear it in a conservative church, you shouldn't wear it to work.

- *Confidentiality Policy.* If you work with sensitive information or meet with clients, you may need a policy that stipulates what is confidential and the expectations of staff regarding privacy.

- *Travel Policy.* This policy sets forth expectations and values regarding business travel.

- *Computer and Digital Information Policy.* This policy essentially dictates that all electronic information developed by the staff through e-mail, social media, and files related to the organization is the property of the organization.

- *Social Media Policy.* Employees cannot represent the organization on their social media accounts (such as Facebook and Twitter) and should affirmatively state that they do not represent the organization in their thoughts and comments.

- *Honorarium Policy.* If staff gets paid invitations to speak on work issues representing the organization, it is work and the funds should go back to the organization.

- *Personal Use of Organizational Property.* This policy provides personal use rules on telephones, computers, and other property owned by the organization. You can also charge for any copies or faxes done for personal use. This is especially important for groups that lend staff laptops and smart phones.

- *Attorney–Client Communications.* If you have attorneys on your staff, this policy is specific to safeguarding that information.

- *Inclusion of People with Disabilities.* This policy provides guidelines on accessibility and communications to make sure the organization is as inclusive as possible.

If you are developing a new organization, don't feel like you need all of these policies created at one time. Personnel policies definitely need to be established if there are paid staff. But other than that, identify the policies that would be regularly used or that are needed by external folks (like government or foundations) and start working your way through developing a policy that makes sense for everyone.

> Finally, there is no need to create any of these policies from scratch. Get copies from allied organizations and adapt them to your needs.

Section 4

Compliance with Government Requirements

Introduction

1. Government Registrations
   - State Incorporation
   - Federal Employer Identification Number (FEIN)
   - 501(c)(3)
   - Charitable Solicitation Registration
   - Sales Tax Exemption
   - State Unemployment

2. Legal Requirements for Staff
   - Hiring Forms
   - Employees versus Contractors
   - Exempt versus Non-Exempt, Comp Time versus Overtime
   - Payroll Taxes
   - Workers' Compensation
   - Disability Insurance

3. Audits

4. Tax Form 990

Introduction – Ethics, Organization, Accountability

There are so many requirements to follow as a nonprofit organization! As one board member put it, "it's like running a small business."

Yet the consequences for weak governance can be serious. It's very important to ensure that your organization is meeting all of its legal requirements. Any holes in your organization's legal compliance can be very difficult to overcome if you ever have to deal with a legal issue.

Legal requirements aside, this is another area where small nonprofit organizations can model practices on how organizations should be run. Ethical behavior and judgement are values that many organizations aspire to in their compliance. As required by the law, organization and accountability are important in working collaboratively with lots of parties – in this case, the government.

There are a number of checklists and resources online for starting a new 501(c)(3) nonprofit organization.

This section explores the government, staff, and financial requirements for keeping your organization going strong.

Chapter 1: Government Registrations

A number of registrations need to be completed with the government at the federal and/or state levels for your nonprofit organization. You can't do much without a few of these!

State incorporation

Filing articles of incorporation with your state is one of the first steps that a new nonprofit organization needs to move toward 501(c)(3) tax-exempt status. Incorporation is important because it shifts personal liability from its founders to the organization as an entity. It is also required to apply for tax-exempt status.

The laws on incorporating an organization vary by state, so look up your state's procedure on the Secretary of State Web page or call the Secretary of State office. You will need to fill out a form or write a set of "articles of incorporation" and file those with the appropriate agency.

Here is what is generally required to incorporate a nonprofit organization:

- Organization Name

- Contact Person and Office Address. Should be a street address, not a post office box, and include a person related to the organization that can receive mail at that address.

- Purpose. A not-for-profit, charitable organization.

- Directors or Trustees. Most states require at least three individuals.

- Incorporators. These can be your founding Board of Directors.

- Bylaws. Your organization's rules.

You will need to pay a filing fee. You will also have reporting requirements with the state, so find out what those are and make a note to complete a report every year.

FEIN number

A Federal Employer Identification Number (FEIN) is a nine-digit number that the IRS assigns to business entities. The IRS uses this number to identify taxpayers who are required to file various business tax returns. It is sort of like an organization's social security number.

Applying for this number is one of the first things you must do to establish your nonprofit organization. You need the FEIN number to do such things as:

- Open a bank account

- Apply for tax-exempt status

- Pay taxes

- Apply for state and government funding

- Hire employees

The application for an FEIN can be done online here: *www.irs.gov/Businesses/Small-Businesses-&-Self-Employed/Apply-for-an-Employer-Identification-Number-(EIN)-Online.* To complete the application, you will need your organization's incorporation date, business address, and business mailing address (if it's different). It's free.

Once you apply, you can get the FEIN right away. It will take as long as four weeks if you mail your form to the IRS.

Federal Tax-Exempt Status 501(c)(3)

Once your organization has received its incorporation as a nonprofit organization and its Federal Employer Identification Number, it can apply for federal tax-exempt status.

Most small nonprofits are tax-exempt (or have tax-exempt status) under the 501(c)(3) public charity section of the IRS tax code. This means that all of the organization's activities have exclusively educational and/or charitable purposes. Contributions given to a 501(c)(3) organization are tax-deductible, so it's an attractive benefit to anyone who wants to give money to your organization. You can also apply for bulk mailing rates, and being a 501(c)(3) makes your organization eligible for foundation and government grants.

There are a couple of other ways to file your nonprofit depending on your activities. The most common alternative is a 501(c)(4) organization. This organization's purpose is to promote the common good and general welfare of the community. It's a good fit for organizations that are actively lobbying on issues. This type of organization is tax-exempt (doesn't pay taxes) but not tax-deductible for donors. Some groups create affiliated 501(c)(4) and 501(c)(3) organizations, such as Bread for the World and the Bread for the World Institute or Jobs with Justice and Jobs with Justice Education Fund.

501(c)(3) organizations can lobby. Federal law regulates how much lobbying can be done, and there are state laws on reporting and disclosure of lobbying. The laws are pretty straightforward, so take a look at the laws before starting any kind of lobbying activity.[1]

In order to be eligible for 501(c)(3) status, an organization has to meet a number of criteria:

- The organization has to be officially incorporated (there are some exceptions for trusts/associations).

- The organization's purposes (as described in its articles of incorporation) all have to fit within the legal definition of "charitable."

- The organization's articles of incorporation need to include a provision stating that if the organization dissolves, the assets will be distributed in a tax-exempt, not-for-profit manner (i.e., the group won't just distribute its remaining assets among its staff or directors).

- The organization can never support candidates for political office.

- The organization must limit its lobbying to an insubstantial part of its budget.

The application for tax exemption can be found at *www.irs.gov/Charities-&-Non-Profits/Application-for-Recognition-of-Exemption*.

Submitting the form is a tedious process. The form itself is very long, and you have to include lots of attachments that describe your organization's activities and pay a fee. If your organization has a partnership with a law firm or law school, you may be able to get it to do the work on a pro bono basis. Having legal help would save you and your leaders some time from trying to figure out how to apply yourself.

However, do not be afraid to tackle the application yourself. Having legal help is not required to fill out the application. If you are willing to commit a few days to just sit down and figure it out, it will get done. And imagine the sense of accomplishment you will feel once it's completed!

Once your application is submitted, it can take a year or more for the IRS to process the application. If there are special circumstances, you can request a faster review from the IRS. After about three months, check on the status of your application and address any problems raised.

---

1. *Public Charities Can Lobby, http://bolderadvocacy.org/wp-content/uploads/2012/06/Public_Charities_Can_Lobby.pdf*

Having 501(c)(3) status gives your organization great benefits but it also brings with it great responsibilities. Once approved, your organization is now responsible for keeping adequate financial records, filing tax returns, giving donors records of their tax-deductible gifts, monitoring and reporting your legislative activity, and obeying other laws required for a 501(c)(3) organization. Make sure that you and your leaders have systems in place to meet these responsibilities before going through the tax-exempt process. Once prepared, your organization will be able to meet the responsibilities and reap the benefits of your hard work.

Charitable Solicitation Registration

Before asking for donations, check with your state government to see if your organization is required to register or obtain a charitable solicitation license. If you need to register, find out whether there are annual reporting requirements or fees (there usually are). These statutes are administered either by the secretary of state, the attorney general, or a separate consumer protection office. The process is usually a simple application plus filing fee, plus annual reports and renewal information.

Most states require organizations that solicit donations in any way (letters, online appeals or events) to register or obtain a license. This includes groups that may not be physically located in the state, but still ask for contributions from the state's residents. The purpose is to protect the general public from fraudulent solicitors. Many nonprofits have to register in multiple states because of their diverse donors.

If you are starting a new organization, apply for your charitable solicitation registration *after* you have your certificate of incorporation, IRS 501(c)(3) statement and business license (if required in your state). You will need to have your organizational bylaws and sometimes a fundraising plan.

Like all registrations, this one is important. Registration is the law, and your organization could be fined if it is found to be out of compliance. If someone unfamiliar with your group receives a solicitation, he or she may contact the state to find out about your organization. If you are not registered, the group not only faces fines from the state, but may also develop a bad reputation with that prospective donor and his/her friends and family. This latter cost can be higher than any fines!

Many states exempt certain types of businesses from this registration. One common exemption is religious groups. If you think your group may qualify, consult with the staff at the state registration office.

Sales Tax Exemption

As a nonprofit organization, you may be eligible for exemption from paying sales tax in your state. If you can gain a sales tax exemption, your organization will save a lot of money when buying items that are necessary to further your organization's work, such as equipment and supplies.

Every state has different requirements to gain tax-exempt status. Do not assume that because your organization is incorporated as a nonprofit or has a 501(c)(3), it will receive this special status. In many states, it is very difficult to get this status – even harder than getting approval for federal tax-exemption! Many states have stricter requirements for what it means to operate for charitable purposes. It is important to show that all the activities of the organization seek that purpose.

In most states, the information you need to apply for a sales tax exemption includes:

- Bylaws
- Articles of incorporation
- Federal Employer Identification Number
- Federal tax exemption letter

You can generally find an application on your state Department of Revenue Website.

If you are approved for an exemption, be sure to check whether or not you will need to renew your application. In some states, you have to renew every five years to keep your exemption. It would be a shame to lose the exemption because you forgot to renew your status!

Once you receive a certificate of exemption from sales tax, make lots of copies and keep them on hand. Then, any authorized person representing the organization can make a tax-free purchase by giving the vendor a copy of the exemption letter. This purchase can only be for the benefit of the organization and cannot be for the personal use of an individual. Having a sales tax exemption saves your organization money when buying things that you need for the work. It is definitely worth the time and energy to fill out the application!

Chapter 2: Legal Requirements for Staff

Keeping up with all of the legal requirements for your organization can be stressful, mostly because it's not always easy to figure it out. Many times groups have gotten into a jam simply because they didn't know what needed to be done.

The information in this chapter varies depending on your state laws, but provides a starting point for federal obligations and where to look on state issues.

Hiring Forms

All new employees should have files created with their names and a number of forms. Those listed below are necessary for payroll and taxes:

- New employee info sheet (by service or with info required by accounting software)

- Direct Deposit Form

- Federal W-4

- State W-4

- I-9 Form

- Copy of ID for I-9 Form

A number of other forms should be included in one's personnel file. Please review the personnel file section of this handbook to find out what other forms should be given to a new employee.

Employees versus Contractors (or "Consultants")

Anyone who does paid work for a nonprofit organization has to be classified as an employee or independent contractor, no matter how many hours that person works a week.

Unfortunately, many employers misclassify their employees in order to save money or the "hassle" with taxes, even though it is against the law.

One church employed both employees and contractors. The pastor was paid as an employee, and all others were paid as contractors and vendors to assist with the church's capital repairs and keep everything running smoothly. One of those classified as a contractor was the assistant to the pastor. She had been employed as a contractor by the church for several years at that point. When asked about why she wasn't an employee, a board member responded that it would be too expensive to pay her taxes and benefits as required by the larger church body. It was a tragic decision to put budgetary considerations first. And it was illegal.

> It is very important to know if your organization needs to hire (or has hired) employees or contractors and to make sure each is classified correctly.

The IRS has lots of info to help make this determination, but the comprehensive guide is 160 pages long.[2]

Instead, take the mirror test. Nancy Leppink, former acting wage and hour administrator with the Department of Labor said the mirror test is where you look in a mirror on the way to work and consider your job. If you think:

> *I am going to work for myself.*
> You are an independent *contractor.*
>
> *I am going to work for someone else.*
> You are an *employee.*

2. *www.irs.gov/pub/irs-utl/emporind.pdf*

The IRS provides three control measures to think about regarding classification:

Behavioral Control

Does your nonprofit control how the worker does her job?

An *employee* would receive direction and support from his/her supervisor, in some cases being told how to do the work.

A *consultant* would be considered an expert. The person is usually self-employed, part of a larger consulting group, or contracted through another nonprofit or business (i.e., not a student right out of college without a business card!). The scope of work or outcomes may be presented, but the person is expected to function independently to accomplish the work. Consultants who often work with nonprofits might be contracted on strategic planning, major gifts, or marketing and are not usually questioned on how much they've worked or how they have spent their time. It's much more a conversation about what needs to be accomplished, what he/she needs to do the work, and deadlines around work product.

Financial Control

Does the business have a right to direct or control the financial and business aspects of the worker's job?

An employer determines an *employee's* salary and how often that person is paid. Appropriate business expenses should be reimbursed per the organization's policy or should be paid for directly with a company credit card.

A *consultant* sends invoices for hours worked and receives payment. He/She might cover business expenses or get reimbursed for such expenses as defined in the contract with the organization.

Type of Relationship

How do the worker and nonprofit leadership interact?

An *employee* has a job description and must abide by the organization's personnel policies and procedures. The person has organizational business cards, is in the staff directory, and usually participates in other areas of the organization as part of the overall team.

A *consultant* has a written contract indicating scope of work, salary, eligible expenses, and timeframe. The person has independent business cards and is not covered by the organization's personnel policy or union contract.

Many employers call their employees contractors illegally. The main reason for this is that it's cheaper, because employers don't have to withhold employment taxes (income taxes, social security, Medicare, and unemployment taxes) for contractors. The burden is on the contractor to make these payments. In some cases, it also allows employers to have less personnel to receive the benefits and other perks outlined in the personnel policy or union contract. Some have also said that it's easier to manage money without the burden of having to raise enough for a consistent payroll.

Nonprofit employers should be very careful to classify all staff appropriately. It is possible to have regular contractors you hire, but most of those doing core program work with no time limit are likely really employees. There are lots of reasons why this is important. The big one is that your organization can get into serious trouble with the government and have to pay back taxes and fines for breaking the law. It is a dishonest and harmful way to run a nonprofit. Your leadership shouldn't be making financial ends meet with short-term financial commitments and shouldn't be cutting corners by not paying taxes. It's also not good for the people who work for you. Working under short-term contracts with no benefits and no job stability is stressful. Staff members also get the burden of paying more taxes as contractors, which can be a lot of money.

Exempt versus Non-exempt, Compensatory (Comp) Time versus Overtime

The other "biggie" in terms of employee classification is to know who is exempt and non-exempt from overtime pay. Exempt employees work as many hours as needed and don't receive overtime pay for working more than 40 hours in a workweek. Non-exempt employees get paid at least 1½ times their rate of pay for every hour more than 40 hours in a workweek.

This is governed at the federal level by the Fair Labor Standards Act (FLSA), which is enforced by the Wage and Hour Division of the Department of Labor.[3] There are also many states with overtime laws, so be sure to check the Website of your state Department of Labor for state laws.

Some incorrectly believe that all salaried employees are exempt from overtime. FALSE. How you are paid doesn't have any bearing on whether you get overtime. Salaried employees can be non-exempt, and hourly employees can be exempt.

In most very small nonprofit organizations, professional staff with significant independent decision-making authority is exempt. However, as the organization grows and adds administrative staff, many of them will be covered by overtime provisions.

---

3. *www.dol.gov/whd/overtime_pay.htm*

Defining Exemption

Generally, the factors that determine exemption include all of the following:

Roles and Responsibilities of the Job. The job title is not as important as the job duties within the organization. If the roles and responsibilities are primarily spent in the following categories (i.e., 80 percent of time or more), then the employee is exempt:

- Executive

- Administrative (only those with decision-making authority)

- Professional – Learned

- Professional – Artistic

- Computer-Related

Exempt positions would include Executive Directors and other senior management, community organizers, program staff, social service providers, and other project managers.

Decision-Making Authority. Does the employee have authority and autonomy to make decisions of significance? This is a difference between managing a project and accomplishing tasks set forth by someone else, inputting data versus managing staff, and committing the organization to a contract or project versus doing secretarial work for a new project. In small nonprofits, all staff members often have varying degrees of independence and autonomy in their work portfolios. But there might be part-time bookkeeping or administrative support that is non-exempt and provides operational support to the organization.

Money Made. Exempt employees must earn at least $455 per week to be exempt from overtime.

Once you've reviewed these factors for each of your organization's positions, mark each job as exempt or non-exempt in the job description and job posting. New hires will want to know if they qualify for overtime. It also means that each position is objectively classified, and unless there's a big change in the duties and how they are carried out by an individual, the job description doesn't need to be reviewed or changed often.

For current staff, make sure non-exempt employees have approval for overtime *before* it happens. Overtime can be a real budget buster, but sometimes it is necessary, so require approval so that the director or manager can keep an eye on payroll expenses. Although don't forget: If the employee works overtime without permission, you have to pay him! If that becomes a pattern, it would be a cause of disciplinary measures for not abiding by the organization's policies.

Also set up strong systems for tracking hours and overtime/comp time. Employees should complete their timesheets recording their hours, and staff supervisors should be sticklers for correct and timely timesheets. Outside of tracking hours and overtime, these records can be terrific indicators of when employees are working too much or too little. Keep strong paper records of timesheets and supervisor approval to pay for any overtime or comp time hours. Your payroll service or accounting software (if you do payroll in house) should also reflect the hours on the the employee's paystub.

If a staff person is working too much, it could be a lot of overtime or comp time, which is costly for the organization. It also results in low morale and general dissatisfaction with job, as it's hard to do a good and thorough job with an eye always on the clock. A consistently high timesheet should be a flag to the supervisor to talk about workload and see if there might be things that can be repriori-

tized or removed from the person's plate.

If a staff person is working too little, that is also an issue. Salaried employees are paid for a minimum number of hours of work, so they can cost the organization money. There is also generally too much work to do at most organizations, so an underworked employee generally means there is an overworked one. This imbalance can create tension between colleagues.

Overtime

Non-exempt employees who work more than 40 hours a workweek must be paid the overtime premium, which is 1½ times the hourly rate of pay. Overtime work should always be approved, in advance, by the staff supervisor to ensure that the organization stays within budget.

Compensatory Time

Compensatory (comp) time is a sticky issue in many workplaces. Comp time is not required by law for exempt employees, but it can be an important perk and incentive for employees working unusual and long hours.

Many organizations intentionally don't have a formal written policy, choosing to provide employees with discretionary comp time as dictated by the director. This is done to prevent abuse of the policy and so the director can keep tabs on when staff is working a lot and needs some time to recharge.

Consider having a policy that toes the line between giving time for lots of hours but does not give too much work that never gets done. Give a short timeframe (since it's meant to help staff recharge rather than provide additional vacation time). And for big organizational events when all hands are on deck and there is lots of work, provide the same amount of comp time after the event is over.

All hours worked and comp time taken should be recorded on timesheets. Supervisors should keep an eye on consistently high hours. If comp time is being taken all the time, the employee probably has a workload issue and the supervisor should meet with that person to see the kind of help that is needed.

For non-exempt staff, it is illegal to substitute comp time for overtime pay, even though it might be an attractive solution for cash-strapped nonprofits.

Payroll Taxes

Paying your employees properly, with correct classification and accounting legally for wages and taxes, is extremely important. Mistakes in this area usually cost your organization money, which is bad. No individual wants to spend time fixing tax issues with the government.

Payroll Service

The easiest way to process payroll is to hire a payroll service. There are so many nice things about these services, such as:

- Experts can help with payroll questions, employee/employer taxes, any deductions needed (e.g., for health care and retirement), and government reporting. These issues can be so daunting and change often.

- The payroll service handles quarterly and annual tax filings.

- An online platform allows you to process payroll remotely (so nice if you are on vacation and a pay period is up!).

- Information about employees, such as hire date, salary levels, old W-2s, and records of any deductions or changes made in the system, is easily accessible.

- Online services can be made available to multiple people in the organization to ensure that there is no payroll theft.

- When a service does your payroll, it reduces your organization's liability for any problems with payroll and taxes.

- The service can handle other related HR functions such as recording hours, vacation and sick time (though normally for greater cost).

Several vendors provide payroll services, including Paycorp, ADP, and Paychex. Some banks also provide these services. Shop around and see which product works best for your organization. **And don't forget to negotiate pricing!** A lot of fees in the proposal can be waived or lowered to keep costs down.

Doing Payroll Yourself

If payroll has been set up already, is almost always the same each pay period (i.e. employees are all salaried at set rates and never need/aren't eligible for overtime), and has been reviewed and given the okay by your auditor or accountant, it might make more sense to do payroll yourself.

Make sure your accounting software has a payroll module that is user-friendly and easy to use. Software is needed to provide a guide through all the payroll issues.

The payroll system should have:

- Withheld employer taxes (federal, state, and city)

- A way to make payments on those withholdings

- A way to report on those withholdings to the government

- A way to provide W-2s and 1099s to staff and contractors

- Any voluntary payroll deductions for health care, retirement, or union dues

Anyone paid more than $600 in a calendar year needs a W-2 form (employee) or 1099 form (contractor).

A challenge on doing payroll yourself is keeping up on the tax filings. Be sure to pay taxes and report to the government on time. Your organization can quickly get into trouble for not making timely tax payment and sending quarterly tax forms. Have someone who really gets this stuff, perhaps a board member or friendly auditor, to review it occasionally and help you to make sure there aren't any problems.

If you are setting up payroll for the first time, get some help from an expert for setup. It's worth some money to make sure you understand all the components of payroll and have it started right at the beginning. It can be an expensive and time-consuming mess to have to go back and fix things later.

Workers' Compensation and Short-Term Disability Insurance

Many states require employers to have workers' compensation, and a handful are starting to require short-term disability insurance for employees. These two types of insurance are beneficial to employees as they provide much needed support in case a person is injured or disabled.

Workers' Compensation

This type of insurance covers employees who are injured or receive an occupational disease on the job. If your organization has an employee who experiences an injury or disease on the job, the organization's workers' compensation policy will provide benefits to that employee. This insurance is very important because your organization is unlikely to have the financial resources to pay for the expenses for an employee injured while at the workplace.

Workers' compensation laws vary widely from state to state, so check with your state Division of Workers' Compensation or Workers' Compensation Board to examine the requirements for nonprofit organizations. In some states, like California, all nonprofits must carry workers' compensation even if they only have one part-time employee. In other states, like Texas, most private employers are not required to provide workers' compensation for their employees. There are also varying requirements for covering volunteers in workers' compensation policies.

Similar to other insurance policies, shop around before purchasing workers' compensation insurance. Your organization may join other nonprofit organizations in your community and buy a policy as a group. Otherwise, get quotes from any reputable and licensed insurance carrier. Most of the well-known carriers, such as CNA and Liberty Mutual, sell workers' compensation insurance policies. Some states (e.g., North Dakota, Ohio, West Virginia, Washington, and Wyoming) have a state agency that sells all the workers' compensation insurance in the state.

> Regardless of your state laws, workers' compensation provides benefits to your employees and protects your organization from difficult situations that may occur if an employee is injured while at work.

To read more about workers' compensation, particularly how the laws differ from state to state, check out *www.workerscompensationinsurance.com.*

Employer's Liability Insurance

Most folks call employer's liability insurance Part 2 of workers' compensation insurance. It essentially protects the employer from claims that the employer was responsible for any injury, illness, or death. This is for economic losses not covered in workers' comp coverage.

In most cases, employer's liability is included in an organization's workers' compensation policies. Just check to make sure that you have this coverage and that the limit is reasonable (at least $50,000, although $100,000 per employee is better).

Short-term/Long-term Disability Insurance

Disability insurance compensates workers for lost income in the event of a disabling injury or illness. This is a shockingly common occurrence. One in four Americans in the workforce will suffer a disabling event before retirement.[4] It is a generous benefit that covers all kinds of ailments such as maternity leave (although one could argue that being pregnant is not a disability!), mental health issues, and physical conditions. It is not a benefit that employees want to use; no one wants to be disabled, but things happen, and it's a way of protecting the long-term physical and financial well-being of employees.

The cost of disability insurance varies widely depending on the employee's age, gender, type of work, and salary. This is an area where an insurance broker should be tapped to help get quotes and find the most affordable option for disability insurance. Some companies provide several types of insurance, such as dental insurance and disability, and buying both from one place can improve the rates.

Most companies won't cover employees who are not full-time workers, or work at least 30 hours a week. Employees are encouraged to accrue 15 sick days so that the elimination period is covered for short-term disability. Of course, vacation time can be used if there's not enough paid sick time. Most of the burden to apply for this insurance is on the employee. She needs to be very diligent in filling out the forms and having the appropriate doctor's permissions in order to get the benefit.

Some states, such as New York, require that employers provide short-term disability insurance, either through a private company or state fund. Check your state's requirements to see if disability is required in your location.

An important case can be made for purchasing disability insurance even if your state doesn't require it. In many workplaces, it has been a literal lifesaver for every person who has needed to use it. It is responsible and ethical to provide this type of long-term coverage when unexpected calamities happen to staff. And in the sphere of benefits, it's not that expensive. It also shows a caring and level of support for fellow human beings that nonprofits should model in their workplaces.

---

4. *www.disabilityinsurance.org/articles/disability-insurance-infographic.html*

Chapter 3: Audits

Many small nonprofits do not want to pay or go through the hassle of an annual audit or financial review. They see themselves as too small to warrant the cost, don't want outsiders looking into their financial records, and don't see the value of having such a review.

Audits can be expensive, but all organizations should have some kind of annual financial review. There are several reasons why this is beneficial to your organization:

- Most foundations require audited financial documents. You need to have financial documents to apply for grants. You don't want your finances to prevent your organization from getting much-needed resources!

- Audits catch errors in the books. Every organization will make mistakes that an independent eye can find and correct.

- Audits assure your board of the overall financial condition of your organization. As the board is fiscally responsible for the organization, an audit can be an assuring record of the success of your organization.

- Audits promote the integrity of your organization's staff. Having an annual audit holds the bookkeeper accountable for his or her work in keeping accurate financial records for your organization.

- Audits can catch theft. Most leaders think theft can't happen to them, but it has and it's important to be prepared for that possibility.

- You can improve the organizational structures for your organization. An audit can help you manage finances responsibly and provide ideas on developing strong financial systems.

An audit must be done by someone independent of the organization. Therefore, staff, board members, or long-term volunteers cannot perform the organization's audits because they cannot provide unbiased information. Neither can the bookkeeper or outside accounting service perform an audit.

The audit report is addressed to the Board of Directors as the trustees of the organization. The report usually includes the following:

- A cover letter signed by the auditor.

- The financial statements, including the statement of financial position (balance sheet), statement of financial activity (income statement), and statement of cash flows.

- Notes to the financial statements, as required by Generally Accepted Accounting Principles (GAAP), which might include information about functional expenses, a depreciation schedule, further information about contributions, volunteer services, and other significant information not obvious in the financial statements.

In addition to the materials included in the audit report, the auditor often prepares a management letter or report to the Board of Directors. This report cites areas in the organization's internal accounting control system that could be improved.

Some nonprofit organizations are legally required to have an annual audit. These organizations spend more than $500,000 in direct or pass-through funds from the federal government or are required by their state laws to do so. In any state where you raise money, your Secretary of State office or Office of the Attorney General can tell you if you are required by the state to have an audit.[5] It is usually for nonprofits that receive contributions over a certain amount.

If your organization is too small to warrant the cost of a formal audit, hire a CPA to conduct a more limited financial review. This review can be tailored to the needs of your organization but could include an analysis of your financial statements recommendations to strengthen internal financial processes.

This review can cost up to half of the cost of an audit, and some states allow small nonprofits to use a financial review in place of an audit for their state regulations. Some funders may allow this review to satisfy the requirements for audited financial records.

Lots of accountant and CPA firms can do your organization's audit. Ask your Board of Directors, volunteers, and friends from other nonprofit organizations whom they use for their audits. You want a CPA that specializes in working with nonprofit organizations. Nonprofit fund accounting is unique. Get a few names and then shop around because the cost varies widely. Also be certain of an auditor's reliability in sticking to a firm timetable. Because you will send the audit to many different individuals and organizations, you want it completed in a timely fashion.

If you are going to invest the resources, hire an auditor that will complete both the audit and your federal Form 990 and state equivalent. Once the audit is complete, it is very easy for an auditor to transfer the audited information into the federal and state equivalent 990 forms. It will save you and/or board members a lot of time to have the auditor complete this for you.

> After finding an auditor and using the firm for a few years, your board should consider changing auditors. It is good practice to switch in order to get a fresh perspective on your organization's financial records.

Having an independent review, either through an audit or a financial review, is recommended on an annual basis. It will not only assure your leadership and the general public of your financial stability but will also help your organization continue to improve your financial structures and maintain your financial records.

5. *www.councilofnonprofits.org/nonprofit-audit-guide/state-law-audit-requirements*

Chapter 4: Tax Form 990

Federal law requires federally tax-exempt nonprofit organizations to annually file the Federal Form 990, the form that serves like a tax return for the IRS.

In 2008, the 990 got a dramatic revision that not only requires financial reporting, but adds expanded sections on governance that require nonprofit organizations to have written policies and practices to comply with the law. It can be complicated, and if your organization is small or just starting out, you may not have many of these things in place. Luckily, small organizations can file a simpler version of the 990 Form depending on income thresholds.

You Should Be Filing the 990 Form Every Year. Why?

Filing the 990 is required by law. If your organization doesn't file the correct version of the 990, after three consecutive years your organization loses its tax-exempt status. Once your tax status is lost, it's difficult to get it back.

The 990 has also become increasingly important as a nonprofit organization's public record of its stability and activities. Once filed with the IRS, the form can be easily accessed on Websites such as *www.guidestar.org* and *www.fdncenter.org*. Also, any individual can request a copy of a nonprofit organization's 990, and the organization is required by law to comply with that request.

The increased accessibility of the 990 gives it a greater importance as a public accountability tool. Potential funders often research an organization before making a gift to support its work. Members of the media ask for the 990 when doing a story about an organization.

All nonprofit organizations, regardless of size, should find out what kind of information the organization shares and how the information is conveyed to the public.

Who Needs to File the 990?

There are three different versions of the 990, which you file depending on your organization's budget and asset size. All forms need to be filed annually.

990-N	gross income of $50,000 or less
990-EZ or 990	gross income of more than $50,000 and less than $200,000, and total assets of less than $500,000.
990	gross income of $200,000 or more, or total assets of $500,000 or more.

If your organization has an auditor, this is the best person to file the 990. However, board members or staff can also file the form for the organization.

When Is the 990 Due?

The most current version of Form 990 can be found on the IRS Website, *www.irs.ustreas. gov*. From the Website, click on "Forms and Publications," and then "Download forms and publications by Form and Instruction Number," and next look for Form 990.

The form is due four and a half months after the end of your fiscal year. For example, if your fiscal year ends December 31, it is due May 15; if your year ends June 30 it is due November 15. Make sure you file your organization's 990 on time! A failure to file the form can lead to significant penalties and fines that could hurt your organization (and potentially your board members!). If you cannot make the deadline, it is simple and acceptable to get an extension (IRS Form 8868), especially if you want to use your completed audited figures on the form.

Policies Required for the 990

The 990 seeks the following written policies:

- Conflict of interest. The policy that outlines procedures where a relationship or affiliation, especially a financial one, is a conflict of interest.

- Whistleblower. The policy that lays out ways employees can safely report violations of the law around financial resources within the organization.

- Document retention and destruction policy. Outlines which documents, hard copy and electronic, should be kept or destroyed, and how.

What Practices Should My Nonprofit Put in Place NOW to Comply with the 990?

Board of Directors

- Board members should all receive copies of the organization's mission, bylaws, and articles of incorporation, and regular financial statements that are discussed during board meetings.

- Board members, or a smaller committee of board members, should set compensation for the Executive Director. The executive committee should review comparable data for compensation and sets the director's salary in conjunction with the staff annual review.

- Board and key staff should review and sign the conflict of interest policy on an annual basis. This review should require written

disclosures of any conflict that might exist.

- Board meeting minutes should be taken and distributed at every board meeting, both at the general and finance committee levels.

Staff

- Appropriate staff like the Executive Director and bookkeeper should also sign and review the conflict of interest policy.

- Staff should be careful to accurately track income and expenses, and observe which expenses are program, fundraising, or administrative. Most groups spend most of their money on programs, which is good and should be accurately reflected. Also, keep back-up records, in case you ever need them.

- Your organization has to be registered in all states in which you are soliciting funds. This charitable solicitation license has different requirements and fees state by state, so check with your Attorney General's office. There is a question on the Form 990 about being registered, so it is best to register in advance.

Planning for the Future

- Board members review the Form 990 before it is filed. While not law, there are two questions on the 990 that relate to board review, and not having a review process could be an indicator of weak board leadership.

- An audit committee of board members oversees the audit and is responsible for presenting regular financial statements to the rest of the leadership. This committee could be the Finance Committee.

- If your group receives a lot of noncash gifts, you could develop a gift acceptance policy.

Public Disclosure Requirements

The IRS requires all nonprofits to make the 990 form open and accessible to the public. This means that any individual can request to see the last three years of your 990 form. The Website guidestar.org makes it easy to see the filed 990s online, but someone can also come to your office to request the information. Organizations should strive for transparency and put the 990 forms on their Website, mail copies to those who request it, and accommodate anyone who might want to see the form in person.

The nonprofit organization Alliance for Justice has a terrific resource on the details of these requirements[6].

Other Considerations

Many states require that nonprofit organizations file a state equivalent of the 990 form. These requirements vary from state to state, so ask your auditor or appropriate government agencies about the regulations in your state. Once you've completed the federal 990, the state version is normally very simple.

The 990 form is a public document, so be thoughtful about the type of information your organization shares and in what form. Take advantage of the sections of the form that give space for you to talk about your organization's programs and services. It is an opportunity not only to share financial information, but also provide a story behind the money.

At the same time, be careful and cautious about what is shared on the form. Friends and foes can both access these records, so think about how this document could be used to support your work or, conversely, harm it.

Finally, get organized! If you take time to create some filing systems and spreadsheets now, the 990 will be easier in years to come. Create a binder with all the general organizational documents in it, including bylaws, articles of incorporation, board minutes by date, and tax-exempt letter. Keep spreadsheets that track program/fundraising/administration, lobbying (if applicable), or other segmented expenses so you can have a tool to use every year. Keep an electronic folder of documents related to the 990. A good scanner and a detail-oriented volunteer could get everything online and organized in hours, and will give you piece of mind moving forward.

---

6. *Give me your 990! http://bolderadvocacy.org/wp-content/ uploads/2012/10/AFJ_990_paywall.pdf*

Section 5

Finance

Introduction

1. Budget

2. Cash Flow

3. Financial Management and Reporting

4. Internal Financial Controls

Introduction – Transparency, Frugality, Responsibility

Money seems to be one of the most mystifying areas of nonprofit management for staff and board members. Folks identify themselves as "money" people or "not-money" people, and seem content to let the financial handling and budget processes remain in the hands of the few folks that get it.

Well, everyone needs to "get it." Money is power, and the amount of money raised and how it is spent and managed, determine the future of nonprofit organizations.

Organizations with the best financial management have developed systems that align with the following values:

- *Transparency*. Keeping records and money practices open for appropriate staff and board members to access them. This could include giving staff access to financial reports and program budgets. Or providing regular reports to the board, and seeking help if finances are tight before it's a crisis. This transparency also extends to

the public sphere in filing the Form 990, communicating financial information with donors, and having regular financial reviews or audits.

- *Frugality*. Encouraging a culture of responsibility around spending. Keeping expenses modest, regularly reviewing vendors for the most-cost effective products, and making careful decisions about how to manage the organization's budget. It also makes the dollars stretch so that the organization is more financially stable in the future. Everyone in your organization will want to know that the money and time they give to the work is valued and spent responsibly.

- *Responsible Systems*. Organizing the mountains of paperwork into systems that make sense for anyone to both review and keep records up to date.

These chapters look at budgets, cash flow, financial management, and internal controls within the context of these values.

Chapter 1: Budget

A budget is a crucial tool in the organization's financial management toolbox. It provides your best, most educated guess on the money raised (income) and costs (expenses) that the organization will have in a year.

Before starting the budget, be sure to review your organization's strategic plan. If you don't have a plan, then remind yourself of the

board's mid- to long-term financial priorities as an organization. Does the board want to build up a reserve fund or buy a building? The budget should reflect the annual income and expenses as well as reflect the bigger picture of the organization's vision and growth.

Here is an example for a small worker center's budget.

Davis City Interfaith Worker Center   2011 Budget

INCOME

Board	$5,000
Corporations	$5,000
Foundation Grants	$40,000
Government Grants	$30,000
Individuals	$28,100
Religious	$7,000
Organizations	$20,000
Special Events	$15,000
Unions	$5,000
In-Kind Support	$10,000
TOTAL INCOME	**$165,100**

EXPENSES

		NOTES
Equipment	$2,500	Computer, printer/fax, phone, furniture
Insurance	$1,200	$100/month
Meetings and Conferences	$2,000	
Miscellaneous	$1,000	
Payroll - Wages	$95,000	Two FT staff
Payroll - Intern Stipends	$5,000	
Payroll - Health Care/Pension/Disability	$6,000	
Payroll - Employment related taxes	$5,600	
Postage	$1,000	
Professional Expense	$10,000	in kind volunteer bookkeeper - $1000
Printing & Reproductions	$1,000	
Rent	$9,000	in kind $750/month
Reserve Fund	$7,500	
Supplies	$2,000	
Training	$5,000	
Translation	$1,000	
Travel	$5,000	
Telephone	$4,500	$200/mo
Website	$800	
TOTAL EXPENSES	**$165,100**	

Expenses

To develop your organization's budget, start with the expenses. What are the costs involved to accomplish your goals and objectives?

Make sure you have annual goals and/or a work plan before developing a budget. You can certainly put anticipated or recurring costs in a budget without much sense of the work (e.g., staff, rent, or telephone), but it is important to consider additional costs that will be necessary to accomplish the work.

For example, a new start-up organization was looking at different database options and wondering if the best use of its limited resources was to buy database software. The director of the organization said that the goals for the organization included fundraising from the mailing list and building the membership base. Given those goals, a database was an important budget priority.

Make sure to also include the expenses that you receive from in-kind sources. Perhaps your organization doesn't pay rent, gets conference call lines for free, or has access to a nice copy machine for educational materials. Anything you would otherwise pay for should be noted in your budget equally on the expense *and* income sides. Ask the donor what the value of his/her contribution should be and put that amount into your budget. Including in-kind expenses is important for three reasons. One, it shows the full and accurate cost of your organization in the budget. This is important in case you would need to pay for things like rent or printing in the future. Two, it also shows funders that you have community support to cover some of these essential items. And three, it acknowledges the donors that provide in-kind support to your organization. This acknowledgment helps deepen these relationships and could help continue this support in the future.

Income

Once your expenses are calculated, approach the income side of the budget. This should be done with the people who do the fundraising. Think about all the different ways that your organization can raise money. It is most helpful to have developed a fundraising plan with goal numbers and strategies that will work (see fundraising section for how to make a plan), but even if you haven't done that yet, give estimates of how much you will be able to raise to cover your expenses.

And don't forget to add in those in-kind sources for your in-kind expenses.

Now here's the tricky part. Your goal is to have a budget where the income and expenses *match*.

Why?

Let's imagine you are a major donor considering making a $10,000 gift to a nonprofit organization you think does really good work. You ask to see a budget and goals from the organization so that you can see the exciting work that will happen with your support.

Scenario A:

The organization has $50,000 more in expenses than income, thus projecting a significant **deficit**.

Your thoughts are that this organization is in trouble. I don't want my money wasted by going to a sinking ship. It will probably have to lay someone off if it doesn't get help quick.

Scenario B:

The organization has $25,000 more in income than expenses, thus projecting a **surplus**.

Your thoughts are that this organization has plenty of money. It doesn't need mine. And I thought nonprofits weren't supposed to make profits?

Scenario C:

The organization presents a **balanced** budget of income and expenses, with 10 percent of the expenses allocated to a cash reserve fund.

Your thoughts are that this budget is thoughtful, ambitious, and in line with the program plans staff has shared with me. I'm impressed with the board's commitment to saving toward a cash reserve in case times are tough.

These might be extreme examples but present very common responses to unbalanced budgets.

It is also worth considering the question suggested in Scenario B: *Can nonprofits make profits?* But your organization's extra income is not a profit. It is a surplus. The difference is that the money is not going to those that seek to add to their bank accounts. It is instead extra income that will be used to strengthen the organization and move forward its mission. One group thought they would have to give part of a grant back to a foundation because they had made more money on their annual fundraising event than they had originally projected. (Answer – NO!)

It is a wonderful thing to have such a great financial year! So first, celebrate your fundraising successes with those that made them happen, including volunteers who helped. Then, consider the best plan of action for your surplus. If the surplus is a one-time thing, then put the money in a cash reserve with the goal to have six months of operating expenses put away for tight years. If the surplus has the potential to be ongoing (like that fundraising event that continues to grow every year), then the board and staff should consider putting some into the cash reserve and consider other needs of the organization that can be met, like new staff, upgrading technology, or improving office space.

Once the income and expenses are drafted, there will be some back and forth to get to a balanced budget everyone can agree with. When developing a budget, the intention should be to end up with something that is ambitious, creative, and realistic for the organization to achieve. Is the fundraising diverse, full of tried and true strategies but also some new things? Are the income goals possible, with help? On the expenses, can the work be accomplished with these expenses? Are there things that can be cut or beefed up to make a balanced budget? What are the financial priorities the board seeks to include in a budget (e.g., increased benefits for staff or new and faster computer equipment)?

It is possible that diminished expenses will have an impact on the annual goals and objectives, which will also need to be adjusted to be doable.

Budget Process

The process to develop a budget will take more time and energy than you might think. But give enough time for a thoughtful process and try to engage everyone involved.

Educate all staff leadership on the budget. Give folks an opportunity to provide input about what should be included. Many staff should be involved in developing the budget and working through the process so they can learn budgeting skills. Folks will do better fundraising and manage their expenses better if they've had a say in developing the budget.

Engage the board in budget making. The board has fiscal responsibility for making sure the organization is financially stable and strong, so it needs to be familiar and invested in the budget. The Finance Committee should see a first draft that includes the current year's budget, current year-to-date income/expense statement, year-end financial projections, and the draft of next year's budget. Provide a balance sheet and the goals and objectives that will be accomplished. The committee should provide input and review before the full board is asked to approve the annual budget.

Don't let the board rubber stamp the budget. Board members should understand how the budget was created, all the income/expense categories, and the financial priorities that were included in the document. This education should be done every year to include new board members and to remind experienced members.

However, also be careful to work with the board to prevent major changes. Sometimes boards make dramatic changes to the budget (usually increases) that the staff is not able to reach in the timeframe allowed. This is usually because there are never enough resources to do the work, so an eager board will want to increase fundraising efforts without putting a lot of thought into whether much more money can be easily raised. This can be tricky to navigate, so educate the board on the budget itself and provide an opportunity to develop financial priorities that can be slowly incorporated into the budget over time, with a great deal of board help. Of course, if you win the lottery and get a bunch of money right away, you can hold a meeting and revise the plan accordingly.

Because the budget process can be lengthy, start developing the budget two to three months before the end of the current fiscal year so that it can be approved before the budget year itself begins. Many organizations' fiscal year runs from January to December, but they don't start making a budget until January. It's too late! By the time the budget is approved, it's February and the group is scrambling because two months have already passed and there's so much work to be done. Develop a process that starts before the end of a fiscal year and is ready for final approval by the board at its last meeting of the year.

An early budgeting process will also be helpful for drafting grant applications. Many foundations seek the current year and next year's budget in their applications, so having a thoughtful budget will be useful for fundraising.

Budget Review

The budget is not a tool that is developed and put on a shelf. Your organization should check in on the budget regularly. The board should review year-to-date income/expenses versus the budget reports at every meeting. The Executive Director and senior staff should be familiar with the budget and review it at least once a month to keep up on fundraising efforts and ensure that everyone stays within budget.

The budget is a tool but not one that should be easily changed. Since a budget is your best guess, sometimes things change during the year and there's a tendency to want to go back and change an approved budget. Unless you have a significant change (more than 20 percent change in any income or expense category), keep the budget as is and reflect the changes in the financial reports to the board, year-end financial projections and in a notes column on the budget worksheet. Too many versions of budgets get confusing for staff and board.

An exception to this rule would be budgets that are being funded by government or foundation grants. You must follow their rules about budget modifications and ask permission if needed on getting budget changes approved. You would need to do this in cases where you want to spend their funded money differently than how you proposed in your grant application. Normally, it's not a problem to get changed, but do it before your financial reports are due, so it doesn't look like you are mismanaging your money.

Good review procedures will lead to the creation of better budgets every year. Budgeting the first year for a new organization can be intimidating. It feels like an important document you are just making up! Be sure to use the financial tools at your disposal to make budgets better and better each year. Have a final financial analysis of the current year's budget versus actual income and expenses. Go through each category and see where you were under- or over-budget, and give reasons why, and if that will happen again. Financial reports are the building blocks of your organization's financial history, so use those blocks to build a stronger and tighter budget for the future.

Chapter 2: Cash Flow

The budget helps you project your income and expenses. But the budget isn't the right tool to manage the cash you need in order to operate on a day-to-day basis. Many organizations have accurate budgets and strong fundraising plans, but the checks don't bring in enough regular cash to pay the bills; thus, payroll is difficult or bills are held until the next grant check comes in.

To manage cash, the best tool is a cash flow worksheet. The worksheet should be organized to show the incoming and outgoing cash on a monthly basis for a 12-month period. It should be a tool connected to the organization's fundraising plan and actively managed and updated by the person in charge of accounting and leadership that manage the money.

Accounting software programs like Quick-Books have template cash flow worksheets that might be useful to give cash flow history. But these worksheets don't project cash flow, so something manually done that shows the past and the future is a better bet.

The following page contains an example of a small worker rights organization's worksheet.

How to Use This Worksheet

The major sections of this worksheet are the following:

Reconciled Bank Balance. The top column is the ACTUAL amount in your primary checking account, the account that should cover the operating expenses of the organization. Be sure that the amount is taken from the online account or bank statement itself.

Income. This is where all the money will come from this year. The cash flow sheet and fun-draising plan and budget should all have the same figures. The income categories should match on the cash flow sheet, fundraising plan (individuals, foundations, corporations, etc.), and budget. The cash flow sheet and fundraising plan should have the same major fundraising strategies that will be done during the year. The difference between them is that your fundraising plan will have realistic goals for each strategy and deadlines for when those strategies will be done. The cash flow sheet will have the amounts and dates for when the money will actually come in from that work.

Expense. This is how your money is spent. There are generally monthly reoccurring expenses, like payroll, rent, phone, or database contract, and then one-time expenses. Again, the expense categories here should match your budget and accounting software expense categories. To make this even more accurate, add a notes column and write in what the money will be spent for and for which program area. For example, that $2,000 expense in equipment might be for a new laptop and printer. Or $600 in printing in September for the year-end fundraising appeal. This information is also helpful for developing a strong and accurate budget.

Running Cash Balance. This bottom row is how much cash you have left. It adds the income raised plus the bank account balance, minus the expenses made.

Like many financial tools, the cash flow worksheet will never be 100 percent accurate, especially in the first year. Sometimes you will get an extra grant you didn't anticipate or lose a major donor, and it can muck up your cash flow projections. Just make an educated guess on what you think will happen. Then

Davis City Interfaith Worker Center
2011 Cash Flow worksheet
updated January 2011

	January	February	March	April	May	June	July	August	September	October	November	December	Total
Reconciled Bank Balance	$32,761.54	$24,936.54	$16,711.54	$6,286.54	-$6,938.46	-$4,363.46	$8,861.54	$17,886.54	$22,911.54	$33,936.54	$33,211.54	$37,986.54	
Income													
Board													$5,000
ask to all members	$2,500												
second ask - before end of year												$2,500	
Corporations													$5,000
Google grant				$5,000									
Foundation Grants													$40,000
Local Community Foundation											$10,000		
Ms. Foundation for Women					$10,000	$20,000							
Government Grants													$30,000
OSHA Grant								$15,000		$10,000			
NIOSH Grant												$5,000	
Individual Gifts													$28,100
Spring Mailing				$5,100									
Year End Mailing											$5,000	$5,000	
Major Donors													
Mr. Gonzalez					$5,000	$5,000							
Ms. Smith													
Ms. Shah									$3,000				
Religious													$7,000
Mailing to religious congregations		$2,000											
Dominican Sisters Grant							$5,000						
Organizations													$15,000
regrant from IWJ							$15,000						
Special Events													$20,000
Gala									$20,000				
Unions													
meetings - 5 unions		$2,000			$2,000			$1,000					$5,000
Total Cash In	$2,500	$4,000	$0	$10,100	$17,000	$25,000	$20,000	$16,000	$23,000	$10,000	$15,000	$12,500	$155,100
Expenses													
Regular Monthly Expenses													
Insurance	$100	$100	$100	$100	$100	$100	$100	$100	$100	$100	$100	$100	$1,200
Payroll	$9,300	$9,300	$9,300	$9,300	$9,300	$9,300	$9,300	$9,300	$9,300	$9,300	$9,300	$9,300	$111,600
Telephone	$375	$375	$375	$375	$375	$375	$375	$375	$375	$375	$375	$375	$4,500
Other Expenses (not regular)													
Equipment				$2,000	$500								$2,500
Meetings & Conferences						$500	$500	$500	$500				$2,000
Miscellaneous					$500					$500			$1,000
Postage		$200	$200	$200					$400				$1,000
Professional Expense		$1,500		$7,500									$9,000
Printing		$200		$200					$600				$1,000
Reserve												$7,500	$7,500
Supplies	$100	$100	$100	$100	$100	$900	$100	$100	$100	$100	$100	$100	$2,000
Training				$2,500	$2,500								$5,000
Translation						$250	$250	$250	$250				$1,000
Travel	$300	$300	$300	$1,000	$1,000	$300	$300	$300	$300	$300	$300	$300	$5,000
Website	$150	$150	$50	$50	$50	$50	$50	$50	$50	$50	$50	$50	$800
Total Cash Out	$10,325	$12,225	$10,425	$23,325	$14,425	$11,775	$10,975	$10,975	$11,975	$10,725	$10,225	$17,725	$155,100
Cash Balance	$24,936.54	$16,711.54	$6,286.54	-$6,938.46	-$4,363.46	$8,861.54	$17,886.54	$22,911.54	$33,936.54	$33,211.54	$37,986.54	$32,761.54	

you can update each month with accurate numbers in order to check-in on your progress and use that information to develop a better picture in the following year.

Interpret the Sample Cash Flow Spreadsheet

So, how do we read and interpret the cash flow worksheet of this organization?

Cash flow is good when:

- Income is diverse, with several strategies spaced nicely throughout the year. Board contributions are high, and a good chunk of the fundraising budget is provided by individuals.

- There is a "holding" expense account devoted to building a reserve fund. This account is not a true expense, but showing the reserve fund in the budget and financial reports prioritizes the financial stability of the organization in the long term.

- There is positive cash flow projected at the beginning of the year. Often small non-profits struggle most in the first quarter of the fiscal year (if using a calendar fiscal year) because many grant checks aren't received until later in the year.

Cash flow becomes a concern when:

- There's a likely cash deficit for the organization in April and May that needs to be addressed. A few ways to address the issue:
  - Let's assume the organization has a $15,000 cash reserve being held in a separate savings account. Money could be taken from here to cover the deficit as long as it is paid back as soon as things are in better shape (although that will reduce the amount of available cash at the end of the year).
  - See if any expenses can be reduced to avoid the deficit. What is the $7,500 professional expense? If that expense could be reduced or eliminated, that would solve the deficit.
  - Move any flexible expenses to other months.

- There's not a lot of cash to work with. The organization spends roughly $13,000/month to cover its budgeted expenses. If only the recurring monthly expenses are paid, that's about $10,000/month. The bank account at its most flush has less than three months in it, which doesn't give much of a cushion. Small organizations should work toward having six months of operating expenses in a separate, reserve fund ($78,000) and four months of operating expenses in its checking account ($52,000) to not have to worry about cash flow.

Best Practices

The cash flow worksheet can help your organization avoid cash flow issues. Here are some best practices to maintain a healthy financial picture:

- *Don't spend money before you receive it.* Folks promise donations all the time, but until that check or online gift gets into the bank account, it's not real. Make sure you get the money promised before spending it.

- Don't wait until you have a crisis. In the example above, certain things could be cut from this organization's budget in order to improve its cash flow. It's better to make incremental cuts that will be sustainable than to wait for a crisis to occur and have to make drastic cuts that will likely include staff.

  Also, staff members have a responsibility to inform the board as soon as an issue is anticipated. Board members don't live and breathe the organization's finances, and need to be given the opportunity and time to help if there is a problem.

- *Don't let individuals (board members, volunteers, staff) lend the organization money in order to pay the bills.* Often folks who want to help think that short-term loans can be a solution. This is not a good practice because it could become a conflict of interest between the person and the organization. It also doesn't help the long-term cash situation of the organization. There is a bigger fundraising and/or budget problem that needs to be addressed, and quickly.

- *Don't spend the expense side of the budget without assuring the income side.* Most staff who don't have fundraising responsibilities are much more comfortable spending money than raising money. Do not allow staff to say, "I want to spend this because it is in the budget." You can spend if indeed the money is in for the income side and available for that particular expense.

Chapter 3: Financial Management and Reporting

Managing your finances is more than just making sure all the money gets deposited and having enough to get employees paid. It's setting up systems and tools that simply, easily, and clearly provide a complete picture of the money that flows in and out of your organization. It's also providing opportunities to staff and board for education and analysis as they are most invested in raising and spending the money.

Your financial management toolkit must include:

- *Budget.* Your tool that sets forth the projected income and expenses of your nonprofit in a fiscal year.

- *Fundraising Plan.* The plan and strategies that show how you will reach the numbers on the income side of the budget.

- *Cash Flow Statement.* When and from which fundraising strategies cash will flow in and out of the bank account in a fiscal year. It is both a record of what is actually happening to the cash and a projection of what the organization anticipates will happen.

- *Financial Reports.* The reports that provide the current data of what is actually happening to the money versus the budget, and a view of what your organization's overall financial health is at any given time.

Other chapters address the budget, fundraising plan, and cash flow statement; this chapter focuses on the bookkeeping and financial reports needed.

First Steps in Bookkeeping

The moment you receive money or need to spend money is when you need to start keeping records of the money – or bookkeeping.

The first thing is to find someone to help you! If there's money, it's pretty easy to hire a bookkeeper on an hourly basis to do your books. Some organizations hire a part-time bookkeeper, and others use an external accounting service. Both are possible depending on the amount of help needed. If your budget is more than $100,000 a year, a professional bookkeeper is money well spent.

Many organizations have a savvy board treasurer who agrees to do the bookkeeping or an independent volunteer (lots of CPAs do pro bono work). Staff can also do the books with oversight from the board treasurer. The person who helps should have good knowledge of nonprofit accounting and be able to develop an easy and consistent accounting and budget structure that will grow with the organization.

Oversight is crucial in keeping accurate books. One organization's accountant was preparing a (non-audit) financial review and mistakenly entered the same expense figures for several accounts for two years. Another softhearted bookkeeper didn't pay quarterly payroll taxes because there wasn't enough money and layoffs would occur if taxes were paid. The IRS took action, and the Executive Director had to inform members and donors that the organization would be in the newspaper due to nonpayment of these taxes.

Next, open a bank account. You need a federal tax ID number for your nonprofit organization, as well as some money to deposit and to complete a bank application. You should get online access and order checks.

Look for a bank account that has commercial no fee checking accounts for nonprofits, services like remote deposit and good online bill pay (even if you don't use it now, you may want to as you grow), and high interest savings or money market accounts. There are different types of banks that vary in terms of community engagement and social responsibility, so consider credit unions or other community banks as good places to put your organization's money. It will take several days to access the money you have deposited, so be sure to leave some time in case there are things you need to pay for right away.

When you open a bank account, the bank may offer to provide you with a debit card. If you plan on using the debit card for deposits, then get one. But it's not a good idea to use a debit card for expenses. One organization had its debit card on a clipboard and staff could sign it out for organizational expenses. The problem is that your debit card pulls money directly out of your account, so there's not as much protection as with a credit card. It's too easy to take out cash and lose receipts, and harder to dispute charges that aren't for the organization. Instead, write checks or get an organizational credit card.

A credit card is a better idea, but proceed with caution. A credit card account can be established under the organization's name and copies of the card given to the Executive Director and other senior staff. You can adjust the credit limits of any individual's card, which is a good idea to limit spending. It is helpful to have a way to quickly buy

something and get points/miles on consistent spending like regular office supplies. However, have a strong procedure on credit card reporting that includes receipts for all expenses made and someone reviewing and approving the statements on a monthly basis.

The next thing is to get some accounting software for nonprofits. The most common programs are QuickBooks, Quicken, or Peachtree. The person who is going to do the bookkeeping should have a big say in which program is chosen. There are online versions of the programs that are a bit more expensive but might be worth it if you need the convenience.

Then, think about accounting structure. The key in structure is to not make things too complicated. The big three to start with are income accounts (where the fundraised money comes in); expense accounts (where the money is spent); and classes (what the money is used for). Income and expense accounts should have the same names and be in the same order in your accounting software, budget, cash flow statement, and fundraising plan. Match the structures so that you don't need to manually change things between documents.

The classes to begin with should be Program, Administration, and Fundraising. These are the three categories that the Form 990 requires for your annual report, so you will need to know figures for each category and can save some time by recording income and expenses by class as you go. If you receive restricted or government grants, you may need to create additional classes based on those grants or the programs that those grants support. If you start using these classes at the beginning of the project, it will be easier to provide financial reports later.

Your structure will need tweaks here and there to make it work for you. So just start with a more basic structure and give yourself some time to make adjustments as needed.

Finally, make sure that the folks within the organization are sharing financial responsibility for the books. The Executive Director should not be the only one entering the transactions, doing payroll, running reports, and presenting those reports to the board. There should be at least two heads (director and board treasurer) with deep knowledge of the finances and a regular review by the board at its meetings. Sharing responsibility will help with ownership of the organization but also more easily engage people in raising money and being careful with resources.

Financial Reports

Once the bookkeeping is up and running, the data should be used to show the organization's financial picture with financial reports.

Two important reports for board members to review are the Income and Expense Statement and Balance Sheet.

Income and Expense Report

This report, also called the Profit and Loss statement depending on your software program, shows the actual income and expenses of your organization within a specified timeframe.

The following report is a final look at 2011 for the sample organization.

Davis City Interfaith Worker Justice — Income/Expense Report

	Jan–Dec 11 Actual	2011 Budget	% of budget
Income			
Board	$500.00	$5,000	10%
Corporations	$1,829.00	$5,000	37%
Foundation Grants	$56,250.00	$40,000	141%
Government Grants	$31,513.81	$30,000	105%
Individuals	$19,502.00	$25,000	78%
Religious	$8,522.00	$10,000	85%
Organizations	$20,678.61	$20,000	103%
Special Events	$5,000.00	$15,000	33%
Unions	$200.00	$5,000	4%
In-Kind Support	$10,000.00	$10,000	100%
TOTAL INCOME	**$153,995.42**	**$165,000**	**93%**
Expenses			
Equipment	$614.40	$2,500	25%
Insurance	$1,196.00	$1,200	100%
Meetings and Conferences	$2,421.41	$2,000	121%
Miscellaneous	$311.08	$1,000	31%
Payroll - Wages	$94,225.10	$95,000	99%
Payroll - Intern Stipends	$0.00	$5,000	0%
Payroll - Health Care/Pension/Disability	$5,749.40	$6,000	96%
Payroll - Employment related taxes	$5,323.87	$5,500	97%
Postage	$666.58	$1,000	67%
Professional Expense	$14,166.47	$10,000	142%
Printing & Reproductions	$404.94	$1,000	40%
Rent	$9,000.00	$9,000	100%
Reserve	$5,000.00	$7,500	67%
Supplies	$1,729.22	$2,000	86%
Training	$5,663.78	$5,000	113%
Translation	$0.00	$1,000	0%
Travel	$4,938.56	$5,000	99%
Telephone	$4,471.44	$4,500	99%
Website	$426.98	$800	53%
TOTAL EXPENSES	**$156,309.23**	**$165,000**	
Net Income	**-$2,313.81**		

The first column is the actual money that came into the organization (income) and actual money that was spent (expenses). The second column is the 2011 budget that the staff developed and the board approved for the year. And the third column is the percentage of the budget. This column can be useful in quickly seeing how close the actual figures got to the budget and can be used in the following analysis.

This worksheet is one that should be given to the board at every meeting. It should contain the first column (year-to-date income and expenses, as close as you can get that have been reconciled with the bank statement), the annual budget, and percentage (if you are interested in looking at data this way). Your accounting software should have a default report that will easily bring up these three columns if you've entered your budget into the system.

In this example, the analysis of this sheet should be a review of what happened in the year and the successes and challenges that the nonprofit faced versus its budget.

Staff and board should ask these three questions in reviewing an income/expense statement. What's good? What's bad? What needs to be flagged in both good and bad in the future?

What's good?

- Income: Exceeded budget goals in foundations, government grants, and organizations.
  - Flag: Were these increased gifts a one-time thing, or can they be budgeted again in the future?

- Expenses
  - Some money was put into the reserve this year. It's not as much as budgeted, but every little bit helps.
  - Some expenses were not as great as anticipated, such as postage and intern stipends. Staff and board worked together to identify and address an upcoming deficit and reduced the deficit by reducing some costs.
  - Increased expense on meetings and trainings could be a good thing. Has the staff increased efforts on outreach? This could increase names on the mailing list, strengthen programming, and improve public reputation. It could be a good use of funds and good for the work.

What's not good? (and should be adequately addressed in next year's budget)

- The year ended in a deficit. It's not a significant deficit, but it still exists and it never feels good to end the year in the red. The cash reserve fund was reduced to cover the gap.
  - Flag: What ultimately happened that caused the deficit? If there were a number of factors, the big ones should be clearly identified and talked about to improve upon in the future.

- Board contributions were WAY lower than budgeted. It looks like the board made a commitment that it did not reach. Funders might think your board isn't committed to the organization.

- Special event income was also extremely under-budgeted. Board members were charged with getting table sponsors and selling tickets.

- Flag: Do both of these challenges have anything to do with broader board issues? Did board members pledge to give help with the event and their gifts and not follow through? Is there a bigger question, like lack of engagement and leadership? Or a need for more education on budgeting and financial management?

- Website spending is also almost half of what was budgeted. This could limit the amount of public outreach done to those that read and give online. How did this expense affect the work? Is it an area that needs to be a priority in the coming year?

The final question on this report is: What is coming up on the horizon? Before the next report, what changes will there be in the financials? Does the board need to help make any of those changes happen? To adequately answer this question related to income, leaders may need the fundraising plan and/or fundraising calendar.

Balance Sheet

This report is also called the statement of financial position, as it shows your organization's overall financial health at a single point in time.

This is the scarier of the two reports, with stiff accounting language and categories and numbers that are not easily explained to nonfinancial folks.

Board members can certainly spend a bunch of time looking through the detail of a balance sheet. Certainly if any financial training is done, it would be good to review an organization's balance sheet as a core part of that training. It is helpful to have at least one board member who really gets this stuff. However, when the financial report only gets 20 minutes on the agenda, and things are generally doing okay, board members should look for a few key markers on the balance sheet:

Assets = Liabilities + Equity

This formula is Balance Sheet Reading 101. A few definitions on what these mean:

1. Assets

Assets are the things that are owned by nonprofit organizations. For small groups, this is mostly cash (the balance in your bank accounts) but you might have other things that have value and could be converted to cash if needed.

Just like with the income/expense statements, the reports that are run for board members should be reconciled with the bank statements, so make sure your bank balances are reconciled monthly, and that board members don't review statements that haven't been reconciled.

2. Liabilities

Liabilities are the things that are owed, or debt. It can be short-term or long-term debt. The person who does your books needs to make sure that any payables are entered into the books.

3. Equity (or Net Assets)

This is what your organization owns, or what it is worth when you subtract what you have (assets) minus what you owe (liabilities).

Davis City Interfaith Worker Center	Balance Sheet
	Dec 31, 11
ASSETS	
Current Assets	
Checking/Savings	
1001 · ShoreBank	43,893.24
Total Checking/Savings	43,893.24
Total Current Assets	43,893.24
TOTAL ASSETS	**43,893.24**
LIABILITIES & EQUITY	
Liabilities	
Current Liabilities	
Accounts Payable	
2000 · Accounts Payable	28,086.20
Total Accounts Payable	28,086.20
Total Current Liabilities	28,086.20
Total Liabilities	**28,086.20**
Equity	
3000 · Opening Bal Equity	4,337.35
32000 · Unrestricted Net Assets	13,783.50
Net Income	-2,313.81
Total Equity	**15,807.04**
TOTAL LIABILITIES & EQUITY	**43,893.24**

In this example, if the organization closed and needed to be liquidated, it would have to use the money it has $43,893.24 less the money that is owed $28.086.20, leaving $15,807.04. But the equity section gives more detail on that amount as what the organization owns, which includes the amount of money originally put in the bank and the leftover money after paying the liabilities. It also subtracts some negative net income, which is the amount at the bottom of the income/expense statement. That would need to be paid back since more expenses were spent than money raised.

The balance sheet always balances. (If yours doesn't balance, you have accounting problems that need to be fixed, quickly!) This is because accounting principles say that you have to enter everything into the books in two accounts. You might have negative numbers in your balance sheet, but the formula works because it forces the entries to be consistent and the same in two different places.

The balance sheet tells a lot about an organization. For small groups, an important thing to use it for is to calculate the Days Cash on Hand.

Days Cash on Hand

It's always helpful to know how many days you can pay for things before running out of cash. Your cash flow statement will provide this information in a much more detailed fashion, per month, but if you want a quick look at the days themselves, this formula can be used.

Total Available Cash/(Annual Cash Disbursements/365) = Days Cash on Hand

In the example, this would be:
$43,893.24 / ($156,309.23/365) = **102 Days Cash**
bank acct balance   2011 expenses/days of year

This organization doesn't have a cash reserve, so while having more than three months cash is good, it's all it has. This would be a much better scenario if there were a cash reserve in addition to the active bank account balance.

But a bit over three months isn't too bad, and this assumes actual expenses in 2011, which may have changed. The organization will need to continue or step up fundraising efforts, but in the meanwhile bills can be paid and operations continue normally.

How to Manage Your Budget and Money

Once the right tools are put in place, the management and oversight of finances can begin.

Managing your money is much easier when you keep looking at it. So, *check in regularly on the financial reports.* The board should look at the financial reports at EVERY meeting. Don't leave finances until the end of the meeting when everyone is tired (or gone). The reports should be consistent from meeting to meeting, generally a balance sheet and reconciled year-to-date income/expense versus budget report. No one likes budget surprises, so provide consistent and clear information every time.

These reports should be presented by the board treasurer. The Executive Director or other leadership staff should meet with the treasurer monthly to review the finances. The treasurer should send the financial reports to the board before the meeting and report to the full board.

The staff should also be familiar with the finances and do more in-depth financial reviews on a quarterly basis (or every three months). About midyear, take a thorough look and develop some year-end projections, especially if there are already significant differences between what will actually happen and the budget. A couple of months before the end of your fiscal year, use the most updated year-end projections to develop a draft budget for the following year and do any last-minute fundraising needed to get to the best financial picture possible.

One side effect on thorough financial review is that you will *need to make plans for good and challenging times.* If you are looking midyear and you just got notice that you didn't get a $40,000 grant that you had budgeted for (and spent some of), you need a plan to think about what happens if you can't make that up. If you meet someone after giving a workshop and receive a $50,000 check two weeks later, what will you do with that money? A good plan is often easier to develop than a bad one, but it's good to have steps done in both so that the leadership is aware of the plan, and that no one tries to create a new plan that hasn't been thought through carefully.

A *cash reserve* is a long-term solution to financial stability. Create a plan with your board on how you would get to six months operating expenses in a cash reserve. How long will it take to build? Just as in personal budgeting, if you commit to putting money into it, even just a little bit over the course of time, it will add up. You might make an organizational commitment to put a percentage of your budget into reserve every year, such as 5 percent.

When times are good, *establish a bank line of credit* to provide a solution to cash flow problems. A line of credit is an open loan, up to a certain amount set by the bank, which your organization could use when necessary. You can establish a line of credit just to have it in place before you need it. Do it at a time when your finances are strong so you can get a better limit. Of course, you will never want to use a line of credit and accrue more debt, but it's a good back-up plan in case short-term problems like cash flow struggles arise.

Finally, the best way to manage money is to make sure you don't run out of it. So, *don't stop fundraising!* Unfortunately, nonprofits can never, ever stop fundraising. Too many times small nonprofit groups have gotten a big new grant and then stopped fundraising for six months until they realized they would run out of money very soon!

Fundraising, like everything else, ebbs and flows throughout the year. The end of the year, time leading up to fundraising events, or heavy grant deadline periods will make fundraising front and center. But even after you get that big new grant, you need to keep adding folks to the mailing list, meeting with donors, and keep building relationships with people. It's likely you still don't have as much money as you would like, or you want to raise more from some sources over others, so there's always more to do to continue to bring in support for your work.

Resources

Many larger cities and some states have resource centers where nonprofit leaders can connect to classes or low-cost consultants to get help with financial management. Ask your local community foundation or non-profit association for help.

Two online resources for help on nonprofit financial management include:

Carol Cantwell, Fun with Financials – *www.funwithfinancials.net*. A wonderful in-depth website to help everyone learn about non-profit finances. Ms. Cantwell does consulting and is an excellent trainer.

National Council of Nonprofits – *www.councilornonprofits.org/resources/financial-management*. A national network with a number of educational resources on budgeting, financial policies, and internal controls.

Chapter 4: Internal Financial Controls

Developing controls to prevent theft seems to run counter to how some small nonprofits operate, which is generally in a spirit of good intentions, trust, informal procedures, and working really, really hard. So don't do too much to develop complicated controls, but just enough to make it hard for someone to steal from your organization. You might be thinking that no one would ever steal from you . . . but someday, someone will try. It happens all the time.

In small organizations, a lot of recommendations are not easy or possible to do without serious work and/or inconvenience. So here are a few basic things that will help significantly in strengthening the inner workings of your organization:

Make everyone follow the policies and procedures of the organization. If counting cash is always done by two people, everyone needs to follow this procedure from the Executive Director to the new volunteer. A small worker center had a mileage reimbursement policy that required employees to keep a log of mileage that included date, number of miles driven, and purpose of travel before getting reimbursed. While the director was on leave, the other staff discovered that she was processing her own reimbursements without any paperwork and that some of the mileage charges didn't seem right. The staff was angry, not only because of the money spent, but also that the director didn't follow the policy.

Lock up your cash! At least three new nonprofit directors revealed that one of the first things they had to do in their new jobs was lock up the cash. One director said the cash box was unlocked and the cash left there all week, uncounted, until the bookkeeper came to do the bank deposit on Tuesdays. In a week's time, the organization had more than 20 volunteers helping out. Everyone said no one would ever steal, but the director wondered how they would know that if the cash was never counted and always easy to find?

Lock up other stuff that has value. Lock up the checkbook, gifts (checks, cash, and credit card information) from donors, laptops if left in the office, and cell phones. Secure your personnel and payroll records that have employee names, social security numbers, and contact information. If you have anything that would be difficult to replace (projectors, translation equipment), don't make it easy to take! Also, keep the key in a place that few know about and that is not too close to the locked items. Make sure the key is labeled in some way so it doesn't get lost. Getting a locksmith for a locked file cabinet is an expensive and embarrassing way to spend an afternoon.

Keep a close eye on the finances. A few ideas on what a good close eye would look like:

- Schedule a financial review or audit every year, done by a third-party accountant. The accountant should make sure the books are in line with GAAP (generally accepted accounting principles) and nonprofit fund accounting principles. She should also make sure the books are closed every year and provide suggestions to the person doing the bookkeeping on ways to make the internal controls and accounting better and easier.

  The board should review and approve the audit/financial review every year.

- Give the Executive Director, board treasurer, and board president online access to the bank accounts. Each should have a unique username and password. The director and treasurer (if the director doesn't already do the books) should review the bank statement every month to look for anything out of the ordinary and make sure the statement was reconciled with the accounting software. The Executive Director could instead receive the unopened bank statements every month, review them, and sign off on the statements before going to the bookkeeper.

- The board should look at financial reports at every meeting. The reports should be the actual year-to-date income/expenses versus the budget and a balance sheet. It should be reconciled to the bank statement BEFORE being seen by the board.

- Create a check policy that involves others but doesn't make you crazy. The bookkeeper really shouldn't cut *and* sign checks. So you could have two check signers: the director and a board member who is easy to reach. Or you could provide a low limit like $100 in which the bookkeeper can write and sign checks, but anything more than the limit would require a check signer. Also think about requiring two signatures for bigger checks, such as more than $1,000. The bank won't enforce this rule, but it could be good practice that more than one person is looking carefully at larger expenditures.

- Make everyone go on vacation for at least a week at one time, every year. There was a big story in Illinois in 2012 about a comptroller who stole more than $53 million from a small town over a 20-year period. She was finally caught when she went on a longer vacation and her substitute found

a secret bank account in her name! It's not only good for the person going on vacation for relaxation and renewal, but it's also good for the organization to ensure that all of the operations are running smoothly and ethically. Incidentally, it's also good for more than one person to be able to perform the operations within an organization. No one should be irreplaceable (even the founder), and sometimes an absence provides an opportunity to develop organizational (vs. individual) records, procedures, and passwords.

Be prepared in case of emergency. Opposition attacks on social change organizations are on the rise. While these kinds of attacks are a sign of the effectiveness of social change groups it is important to be prepared and ready when they occur. RoadMap, a group of social justice consultants, has put together materials, webinars and tools that can be found at *www.roadmapconsulting.org.* If you feel like your group is vulnerable, it would be worth the time to complete the comprehensive checklist on the organization's website and develop a crisis management plan.

If someone really *wants* to steal from your organization, he/she will find a way to do so. But don't make it easy for them. Good systems and regular review will eventually catch the theft.

Also, having clear policies and procedures reassures staff and board members that the organization values organization, transparency, integrity, and ethical behavior. This is yet another reason why they should want to be involved in your work!

Section 6

Fund Development

Introduction

1. Creating a Fundraising Plan

2. Identifying and Building Relationships with Diverse Funding Sources

3. Thanking Your Donors

4. Staying on Track

5. Fundraising Resources for Small Nonprofits

Introduction – Honesty, Trustworthiness, Appreciation

Fundraising is an integral part of running an effective organization. Internally, so much of fundraising is dependent on good infrastructure. Staff needs to be able to build relationships with donors, communicate with those donors effectively, and show appreciation for donors' gifts. The organization needs to be able to provide accurate and clear financial reports and show how the money is spent in a responsible fashion. Donors want to give to honest and trustworthy organizations that are run with integrity.

The right donors for your organization should also reflect your organization's values. Many of the sources listed below have their own visions, missions, and values. Those values may not align with your nonprofit's, and that means there might be a difficult decision ahead in deciding whether or not to accept those gifts. Nonprofits should be equal partners in the philanthropic process. Ask funders what you need, not what you think funders want to give you.

Chapter 1: Creating a Fundraising Plan

Veteran fundraiser and organizer Gary Delgado says that there are four steps to successful fundraising[1]:

1. Plan
2. Plan
3. Plan
4. Work your plan

A fundraising plan is the strategy to raise the money you need to do the work effectively. It should be completed every year in conjunction with the goals, objectives, and budget for your organization. The Board of Directors should be heavily involved in creating a fundraising plan as it can (and should!) help staff implement it throughout the year.

A fundraising plan should incorporate many different ways to raise money. It is important for the long-term sustainability of the organization to ask lots of different people and organizations to support your work. Also, a fundraising plan should have realistic goals. The staff and board of the organization want to be able to celebrate the fundraising they have done, so goals set should be ambitious but achievable.

Most importantly, the total income proposed in a fundraising plan must match the income portion of your budget. If you cannot raise the amount needed in the budget, you will have to go back to the budget and pare down your expenses.

Step 1: Review the Data
The first step is to look and see what kind of fundraising you've done in the past. Your financial reports should show each income category and how much money the organization has raised in the past. Look at the income detail in the profit/loss report to understand when the money has come in. If you have a database, pull up your donor records sorted by income category.

If your organization is new, but operating, you likely just have a few gifts to review so far. Spend the time looking at the 990s of a few similar organizations in your community. How much money do they receive from foundations? Government? Earned income? This will help you think about ways your organization can build its fundraising plan.

Also look at the most recent Giving USA numbers on where contributions come from.[2] More than 80 percent of giving is from individuals, and another 7–8 percent comes from bequests from donors' wills. Some organizations spend a lot of time and resources writing grant proposals, but make sure there is some strategy regarding where money is given the most.

Then, do some analysis. This is best done with staff and the fundraising committee of the board. What is working? What has the potential for growth in the coming year? What is not working? Are there any gifts that were one-time gifts that you can't fundraise around in the future? What are you currently not able to do that you know works for allied organizations?

The goal in the data analysis is to get your fundraising committee thinking about historical experience and to set realistic goals in your fundraising plan.

---

1. Kim Klein, *Fundraising for Social Change*, Chardon Press Series. 2001.

2. Givingusareport.com

Step 2: Brainstorm

This can be a lot of fun! Hold a fundraising meeting with staff, board and volunteers who want to brainstorm ways to raise money for the organization. It would be good to include all the board in the conversation, so make it an agenda item during a board meeting. Share the analysis you've just done, as well as the history of successful/not-good fundraising, and work together to come up with a list of ideas.

Think about:

Resources of the organization. What does the organization have access to that can be used to help raise money? It likely has people (staff, board, volunteers) and their time that will help, or maybe budgeted funds to spend on printing and postage. But what about other nonmonetary items? Is there a board member with a vacation house that could be used for a silent auction? Or someone with connections to a restaurant that might offer catering for a discounted rate?

Ask board members explicitly about their experience with fundraising or anyone they know who has good experience. Many community leaders have lots of experience and like doing parts of it!

Strategies that are possible given the resources. Once the resources are identified, brainstorm ideas that will raise money utilizing those resources. For example, many people think a big fancy fundraising event raises a lot of money. It is true that many nonprofits hold successful events, but if you've never held one before and you have one part-time staff, it will be very difficult to plan and implement well.

Different strategies for each income category. Make sure you know where every dollar is coming from. One nonprofit had a draft budget but hadn't put any thought into how to raise $5,000 from corporations. Halfway through the fiscal year, the board wanted to know why there was no income yet recorded in that category, and the answer was that there was no plan to raise it. The money will not magically appear if there's no plan for it.

When building a strong development plan, growth is not only dollars raised but also number of donors. People should be encouraged to brainstorm ways to bring in new donors, encourage current donors to give more, and raise more dollars.

The goal is NOT to do ALL of the things the committee suggests but to get creative juices flowing about what the leadership thinks can and should be done to raise money. This is also helpful later because board members are much more interested in working to raise money around plans they created.

Keep a record of all the ideas, regardless of their feasibility. Maybe you don't have the capacity to do a silent auction this year, but might do it in the future. Keep a list of auction items and vacation homes from previous meetings for future solicitations.

Folks who have energy around these strategies. Many times things are accomplished in small organizations because of the passion, interest, and energy of just one person. So there may be a strategy or two that is not possible given staff capacity or money, but might be considered if there's a board member or volunteer willing to lead it. Be open and encourage leadership in fundraising as long as it makes sense and is not troublesome for others.

Step 3: Draft a Plan

Someone who will take leadership on the fundraising should draft a plan given all the information that's been developed.

The key components to be included in a fundraising plan include:

- Income category (foundations, individuals, etc.)
- Fundraising goal for each category
- Strategies to reach the goal
- Date to be completed
- Who will work on them
- Cost for any strategies

Make sure that the income category and fundraising goal match your annual budget. Using the same language, and even the same order, will make things easier when you are reviewing the finances.

A key part of any plan is to ensure that all of the leadership is giving to the organization; 100 percent of board members should be making personally meaningful gifts to the organization. Some organizations require specific dollar amounts that each board member gives, whereas others allow board members to "give or get" a specific amount to support the organization. Staff members should also be invited to contribute. It shows an investment in the organization; in addition, it's difficult to raise money from other people if one hasn't made a personal gift.

An example from Davis City Interfaith Worker Justice (the example organization given in the Finance section) includes the following:

Individuals

Goal: $28,100

- Direct Mail Appeals – Staff – $14,000
  - Spring Appeal (April 1) to donors in last 3 years – $3,000
    - Cost: $250
  - Year-end Appeal (Nov. 15) to whole mailing list – $9,000
    - Cost: $750
  - 6 online appeals – $2,000
    - 2 after mail appeals have been sent;
    - 4 as part of Giving Tuesday
- Major Donor Meetings – Staff and Board Members – $5,000
  - Staff and board generate list of at least 20 new donors who can give at least $250. Add or Tag in Mailing List.
  - Assign each donor a staff or board contact. 1 staff/1 board try to meet with every person (December 1) – $3,000
  - Ask all current donors to make their annual gifts – $2,000
- Launch monthly giving program – Staff – $1,000
  - 5 board members commit to signing up for the program (February 1) – $600
  - Seek at least 5 current or new donors to become monthly givers – $400
- Grassroots Fundraising Events – $8,100
  - Annual Walk Fundraiser (June 15) – $3,100
  - 2 house parties hosted by donors (March and October) – $3,000
  - Labor Day picnic (September) – $2,000

Each income category should be reflected in the fundraising plan, including in-kind gifts.

The fundraising plan should equal the income (and expense) portion of your budget. If it is less than the budget, go back and trim expenses. If it is more, go back and think about modest increases. Or, especially for new fundraising ideas, don't include the goal in the budgetary plans. It never hurts to raise a bit more money than expected! Things will happen during the course of the year that no one can anticipate, so it could provide a bit of a cushion with unplanned expenses.

Review the timing of your fundraising. Look at the strategies and make sure the fundraising is spread out and not all lumped together during one time. For example, don't hold a major fundraising event in a month where four grants are due. It will add unnecessary stress! You also need money coming in all the time. Having fundraising done throughout the year will help with the organization's cash flow. The finance section includes a cash flow worksheet through which you can chart out the fundraising and cash on a monthly basis to make sure all expenses are met.

Make sure that the culture of fundraising in the organization is represented in the plan. Do all staff and board and volunteers have a role to play in the plan? The burden of organizing them might fall to a smaller fundraising committee, but everyone should be helping to strengthen the organization by raising money.

Step 4: Review and Finalize
When the plan is drafted, go back to the folks who brainstormed for review and discussion of the plan template and make sure it works for everyone. Identify who will help with which parts of the plan and figure out a regular reporting system. A few more small changes, and you should be done!

Step 5: Use it!
The plan is not a document to be written and put on a shelf. It's a tool and reference to be referred to and used throughout the year. It can be changed as the plans change.

Review the plan with the staff that fundraises and/or with the board fundraising committee on at least a quarterly basis. Report on any updates to the plan, date changes, and other revisions that have come up. Keep it up to date and it will be a crucial organizing tool to getting the work done!

Once a first plan is developed, it is much easier to update and revise in following years. Take the time to develop something good the first time, so that it's a helpful and detailed tool that can be fine tuned in the future.

Chapter 2: Identifying and Building Relationships with Diverse Funding Sources

If you want money, you have to ask for it. If you ask enough people, you will get it. The word you will hear most often is no, so your success depends on the number of people you ask. If no one has turned you down recently, it's because you haven't been asking enough.

– Kim Klein, author of Fundraising for Social Change

The long-term fundraising success of your organization depends on identifying diverse funding sources that will support your efforts. But where do you start? What tools do you need to be successful? Who can help you? This section focuses on identifying and building relationships with the key funding sources that most commonly fund small non-profit groups: individuals, foundations, and other organizations.

In general, a few basic fundraising principles will guide the approach of each of these funding sources:

- Building relationships and trust with potential donors is **the most important thing** you can do to raise money.

- You must ask to receive. Often, organizations with the greatest need are the most afraid to ask for financial support. People want to help, and you need to give them concrete and easy ways to do so.

- Finding donors is as easy as your ABCs. The strongest potential donors are those who have the **A**bility to make a gift, **B**elieve in the mission of your organization, and have a **C**onnection with someone within the organization. A donor that lacks any of these pieces is less likely to make a gift to the organization.

- Persistence is key. Don't be discouraged by

people saying no. In some cases, "no" really means "at some point in the future." It is not personal to you or your organization. The key is to continue seeking and asking for support. The more you ask, the more you will be surprised by those saying yes.

Individuals

Financial support from individuals constitutes more than 80 percent of all philanthropic giving. Although time consuming, it is imperative that you build a broad base of individual donors for your organization right from the beginning. Building support amongst individuals is so important because:

- Individual donors provide a more stable source of financial support than foundations or other organizations

- Individuals give consistently and for a long period of time

- Building relationships with donors strengthens your organization and spreads its message in the community

- Most individual donors give general support funds that can be used where most needed and are not restricted for specific purposes

- In case of a financial crisis, you can quickly turn to a large number of supporters

The general rule in getting financial support from individuals is the more personal the approach, the more powerful the response. An in-person meeting is better than a phone call, which is better than mail or giving online. It is important to devise a plan that incorporates all of these methods with the goal of increasing the power of your relationship each time. Also, usually the higher the position of the person requesting the gift, the better the result might be. For example, the Executive Director or board member will likely yield more money than junior staff or interns.

Nonprofits should also reflect values of kindness and respect in language used to raise money. Some people talk about needing donors to "cough it up" or they "go after donors" for a gift. As relationships are key to raising money successfully, it is better to use language that treats people as people, not as dollar signs.

You also want to convey urgency and purpose in your message, and be as specific as possible. Do you have four weeks to raise $2,500 to take a bus to advocate for legislation? That's just $25 from 100 people. Ask folks to give just $25, and some who might have never given before. And some will give more than the amount requested. Generosity often comes from unexpected places.

> Make it easy for someone to give, all of the time. That means you should put donation information on just about everything and have simple and streamlined online capacity to take donations.

Consider the following ways to raise money from individuals.

Direct Mail Appeals. These are letters or e-mails asking individuals on your mailing list to give. Some people only give via mail, some only give via e-mail, and others give both ways, so make sure you regularly ask in both formats. The end of the year is the biggest fundraising time of year for appeals, so if you have a limited budget for mailing, this would be the best time to send a letter.

Sending appeal letters and e-mails requires the organization to keep a database and up-date people's information regularly. Remember, more than 36 million Americans move every year, so your data can quickly become outdated.

The best way to develop a direct mail strategy is to build your own internal list of names. Staff and board members should regularly be asked to get their friends, family members, and contacts into the database. They can't give if they aren't asked.

Appeals that are followed up with e-mails or phone calls by people who know the donors will yield a much higher success rate. Appeals that have notes from board members or staff on the letter will also increase gifts. It's even better if the board member writes their last name on the outer envelope, above the return address line.

> Compelling appeals convey passion and a sense of urgency. Provide personal stories and pictures that share the achievements and impact of your work.

Ask for a specific amount, or for a first gift, whatever standard amount seems realistic to your mailing list. Is it $20, $25, or $50?

Don't forget to give folks an easy way to give! Provide a response card with reply envelope in appeal letters and a link that goes to a donation page in e-solicitations.

Ask for a gift in person. A more personal way to ask for a gift, especially a larger gift (typically $250 or more) is to build a personal relationship and asking for financial support in person. The steps for successfully raising money this way include:

- *Build a list*. Ask board members, allies, and others who know people with financial capacity for a list of people who might respond to a request for a meeting. Look through those donors already giving to your organization at higher levels. Figure out who knows whom and give assignments for building relationships.

- *Build a relationship.* Add all these folks to your mailing/e-mail list. Reach out to them by sending an introductory e-mail or letter providing information about the organization and asking for a meeting to share more about the work. Ask the person who gave you the name to introduce you. Get to know the person. Find out what the person is interested in and how the person might want to get involved in your work.

  You might be surprised by who you already know that will support the organization. A recent graduate school student was approached by a friend's dad who wanted to know where she took a job after graduation so he could make a gift to that organization. Friends support other friends, often regardless of the cause.

  Also ask donors for advice. Many of them have been very successful in their careers and have skills and experience that could help your work. It might also be a way to involve the person beyond money. Donors might also know other individuals whom you should meet who would care about the organization.

- *Ask.* Don't ask for a gift at the first meeting, but at a point that feels right, a donor who has capacity to give should be asked in person. When you ask for a gift, you should have a specific request in mind that connects with the interests of the donor. It is usually easier to ask for a more modest gift the first time. If you sense that the person has the capacity to give more than you have asked for, you can make a note of it and ask for a larger amount in the future.

- *Thank you and follow up.* Follow up on any

promises you made during the meeting, such as materials or documents you were asked to send to the donor. Thank the donor promptly after the meeting, regardless of whether you received a gift.

If you did receive a donation, send a tax-exempt letter thanking the person for their gift. Add the person to your organization's mailing list or update his/her record. The gift should be recorded in your organization's database with any special information on the person's interests, priorities, and things you should follow up on in the future. Consider sending the donor regular updates on his/her interests and continue to seek ways to involve him/her in the organization.

If you did not receive a gift, don't be discouraged. Many people have circumstances that affect their ability to give at a specific time. It would be helpful to work with a person who has a connection to the donor or a board member to create a follow-up plan to try again at a later date. This could include keeping the door open by offering to send information or to connect with the individual at a later date. Notes from the meeting and follow-up steps should be recorded in your organization's database.

Although it can often be a daunting task to ask people for money, it does get easier over time. Remember the values and passion you have for your organization's work. Your vision and enthusiasm will make it easier on you as well as inspire people to contribute!

Online Giving. An increasing number of supporters or potential supporters will only give online. Online giving is quick, easy, and cheap, and the gift can be processed within minutes. This is particularly useful for organizations that address urgent issues and need lots of gifts fast.

The frequency and prominence of asking for gifts vary by organization. Some organizations have a giving button on every page of their Website. Others put a giving button on the first page and the contact page only. Determine what feels appropriate for your group.

Most people are overwhelmed by e-mails and e-mail solicitations. Start slowly by doing a follow-up e-mail for every paper direct mail appeal you send, or try a two-week online campaign with a modest goal and several e-mails within a defined period of time that coincides with something in your work.

Your Website should have the capacity to receive gifts quickly and easily. Several companies cater to nonprofit organizations and can provide tools for online giving. Look for a company with modest processing fees that can process your gifts automatically from the Website and that syncs easily with your database.

Social media, another online strategy to raise money, is most effective when it is used by individuals involved with your organization to their friends and family. There are many options in this area such as Facebook birthday or crowd funding sites. Having a specific goal in these fundraising efforts creates urgency and will encourage friends to kick in money, especially in small amounts.

Asking for Support through Outreach Materials. Organizations often ask for financial support as a part of their other outreach materials. Fundraising is not the primary purpose of the materials, but it is often a method to get support from individuals who appreciate the quality and effectiveness of your materials and work. Typically, the fundraising ask is "a soft ask" that does not draw a lot of attention away from the primary purposes of the materials. These outreach materials could include newsletters, organizational brochures, educational pamphlets, or annual reports.

Sending outreach materials is important because it shows that people aren't only hearing about an organization when it is asking for money. Let donors know about the important work and how their money is being put to good use. If these stories inspire someone to make a gift, then they have an easy and convenient way to do so.

Planned Giving. It is never too early to ask those individuals who know and love your work to name your organization in their wills. If your organization is developing long-term goals and financial plans, it would be good to invite all board members and experienced staff members to make a planned gift. Highlighting a donor who has made a gift is also an interesting article in a newsletter and can be used as a way to regularly invite your community to make a pledge to give in this way. If a donor is interested in developing an endowment, talk to your community foundation to see if it's the best option for the organization.

Earned Income. Large nonprofits have done well in raising money by providing services to their members. For example, AAA provides a whole variety of services to its members, from emergency road assistance to auto insurance and discounts on hotels and travel. It also mobilizes their 51 million members on motorist rights and does education and advocacy to promote safe driving.

Earned income could be difficult for some small nonprofits to develop but is worth thinking about if you want to grow your membership and have deep ties within the community. Can your organization provide things that are both tied to your mission and could impact on your community?

Or are there services you could provide that

other area businesses and individuals might pay for? One nonprofit offers translation services for a fee that is widely used by the county court system and other organizations for bilingual meetings. Or can you provide training for schools that would pay for them? Or can you charging a modest honorarium when staff members are asked to speak to organizations or at conferences? Earned income can provide a steady stream of support that also demonstrates how effective a social enterprise can be. It would also improve your outreach in the community and could be a good way to accomplish your work.

Foundations

Grants from foundations can be a good source of income for small nonprofit organizations. Foundations like to "plant seeds" with their grants to support new organizations, new projects, or new issues. This can be a benefit if an organization is just starting out or is embarking on a new, exciting campaign.

Be careful not to rely on foundations as a sole source of support, but rather as one strategy in your larger fundraising plan. Foundations often change their priorities, which can leave an organization scrambling if its issue is suddenly not their priority. Many foundations also limit the number of years they can support an organization, so that support can't be relied upon for long periods of time.

There are a few different types of foundations you should research or inquire about that might fund your work:

Community foundations. These local foundations exist in almost every community in the United States. One big part of what community foundations do is to make grants on behalf of individuals, families, businesses, and others that have set up funds within the foundation for charitable purposes. In met-

ropolitan areas, they may be named after the city they serve, like the Cleveland Foundation. In more rural areas, they may have a county or regional name, like the Benton Community Foundation serving Benton County, Indiana, or the North Georgia Community Foundation that serves 15 counties in northeast Georgia.

Issue-focused foundations. Many foundations in the country focus on a particular issue. Look for those that support your organization's issue. These foundations are often very competitive (particularly the nationally focused foundations), but many could be a source of support for a new program, especially one that could be replicated in other places.

Religious foundations. There are many grant programs through religious denominations, orders, and congregations. These are not usually big grants, but can be reliable sources of funding and engage people from that faith community in your work. If your organization does any work with the religious community or partners with any faith-based organizations, ask about religious foundations in your area and outreach grants from congregations.

Family foundations. These foundations are a way for families to do their own charitable giving. Many of them are quite small and don't have easy ways to access their information (like websites). Ask your board members, friends, and staff of other local organizations about family foundations in your area. Most of them fund where the family lives, so they can be a great local source of financial support. Because families operate them, they are often more long-term and faithful givers than other types of foundations.

Foundation grants can take months to secure, so apply early and with the following process.

Do the Research. Start by developing a list of 10 to 15 strong foundations to reach out to for possible funding.

Talk, talk, talk. If you have current funders, talk to them about your desire to grow your organization and grant income. Ask them who else should be funding you? Who do they know, and could they introduce you through e-mail or coffee? There is no better advocate someone who has already given to you.

Talk to your Board of Directors about new foundations. Do they know anyone who serves on boards or works for foundations? Could they come with you to a meeting? Talk to your friends and colleagues. Who funds similar organizations? Look up those non-profits' Websites to see if there are annual reports or 990s that identify their funding.

Get online. Look up foundation Websites. Note their program areas, deadlines, application processes, and past grantees. Sometimes what foundations say they fund and what they actually fund are different. Foundation Websites are frequently out of date. Sometimes foundations' priorities have completely changed. Other times, foundations have very particular approaches. For example, a foundation might have a program area under job creation, but their funding is all for organizations that provide nurse training classes. Certainly this is job creation but is limited to a particular strategy to achieve that goal.

If grant information is not easily accessible on a foundation's Website, look for the foundation's Form 990s on *www.guidestar. org* or *www.fdncenter.org*. Get its guidelines and deadlines. Look for current grantees with programs similar to yours and amounts of grants. (Do you know its current grantees? Call them and ask for advice!)

Call, call, call. Next, look up the foundation program officer that best fits your organization. Think through specifically how your organization or project fits the foundation's priorities. Call and talk to a program officer about the foundation's current priorities, and whether or not there is a match in the foundation's mission and your organization's project. Try to get a face-to-face meeting with the program officer to build a relationship with the person. E-mail is a good way to ask for a meeting, but be sure to explain why you want to meet and describe your program a little, showing how it's a good fit with the foundation. A meeting is a great way to find out more about the foundation and see if there's an opportunity for funding.

Sometimes the foundation Website clearly says not to call. Pay attention to the Website; you don't want to break the guidelines and annoy the foundation staff. Try to e-mail and ask for a meeting, or just send an e-mail introducing yourself and your program and asking to talk.

Build Relationships. Even though foundations appear to fund programs, in reality they make decisions based on funding people whom they trust to run programs. Thus, foundations must trust the leadership of your organization. They will trust you based on your reputation and relationship in your community. If at all possible, you really do want to meet with the appropriate program officer at the foundation.

Write the Application. Most foundations have a tiered application process that has very specific instructions. The application often has a regular deadline for submission, and initially asks for a letter of inquiry and a few other attachments.

The letter of inquiry, or LOI, briefly describes your program and requests the opportunity to submit a full proposal for funding. It should include the amount of support you would like to ask for. You will know an appropriate amount by looking at the amounts that the foundation has given to other grantees, listed on its Website or 990 tax form.

Try NEVER to send a letter of inquiry without a conversation first. The conversation can give very important clues about what to highlight in your letter. Then, make sure to reference the conversation in the letter. If you do send a letter without a conversation, write in the letter that you will call in the next couple of weeks. THEN DO IT!

Your LOI should be a tailored letter that speaks directly to the foundation, using the language you see on its Website. Use the **same** words it uses to clearly show connections between your work and its priorities.

Your LOI should be in a format that is easy to read. If the foundation asks questions that need to be answered, use those questions exactly as subheadings with the answer underneath. Assume that your reader will skim the letter, so lay it out in a way that will be very easy to read quickly and gain important information about your program.

Most LOIs are sent via mail or e-mail. Keep a hard copy and electronic copy for your records in a folder marked with the name of the foundation. All correspondence with a foundation should be kept in an appropriately marked folder for institutional memory.

If your letter is accepted, then the foundation will ask you to submit a full grant proposal.

The proposal can be quite a time-consuming project, so be sure to look at the foundation's instructions well in advance to make sure you

have enough time to put together the proposal and attachments. Look ahead 60 days before the proposal is due to start it.

The most important thing you can do in proposal writing is to follow the foundation's instructions. A common reason proposals are rejected is that the applicants don't follow directions or meet the deadlines. This is largely because foundations see attention to detail as an indication of how the organization is run and how it will spend its money responsibly. Look carefully at the foundation's requirements and follow them exactly.

The proposal itself should be developed using clear and persuasive language. Your need, program goals, and objectives, and anything else the foundation asks should be presented clearly. The program objectives are the "meat" of the proposal and should be clear and measurable. Your funders want results, and good writing in the proposal will make your grant reporting and evaluation much easier.

Once your proposal is written, have someone with fresh eyes read it! Give it to someone who doesn't know much about your program for a thorough read. Often nonprofit staff use jargon that makes their program more complicated than it needs to be. Your outside reader should read your proposal and understand why your program exists, its goals, and what you will do in the coming year with grant funding. Someone should proofread the proposal because grammatical mistakes are embarrassing and unprofessional. Interns can be a great resource as workers new to your organization and would benefit by learning more about the work.

Financial reports are a key piece of an application that should be done carefully by the organization. If a project budget or 990 Form is required and there are any potential red flags, such as an operating deficit, or a large increase in net assets, provide a narrative with an explanation of the issues.

Every foundation asks for various attachments, often in a particular order. Attach them all as required.

Follow-Up. A few months after you submit your proposal, you will hear from the foundation if your grant has been approved.

If you are approved, call and send a thank you letter. Your program officer is your advocate with the foundation board and has done a lot of work to help you get this grant. The person deserves your gratitude. Then, be sure to provide follow-up reports as required and on time. Most foundations won't give another grant if you haven't reported on your first one!

If you are rejected, call the program officer and ask for feedback. Ask why you were declined and describe ways the proposal could be improved, if it is appropriate to reapply, and when. No matter what, try to keep the door open to a future relationship. Ask to check in at six months to see if things have changed, or meet when you are in town. Invite the program officer to an event in the future.

No matter what the result of your grant application is, be intentional about keeping in touch with funders and potential funders. The program officers and foundation presidents should be on your mailing list. Call staff for meetings when you are traveling in their area, send newsletters and media articles, and invite them to events.

Foundation fundraising takes time and a good amount of persistence. Keep calling, writing, and applying for programs. And be sure to be working other fundraising strategies that will bring in money and build the organization while your applications are in the pipeline.

Government Grants

Grants provided by federal, state, and local governments can provide ongoing crucial support to your organization and its work. The applications can be complicated and time consuming, so be selective in deciding which grant program is worth applying for. The organization must have strong administrative systems and staff capacity to complete the reimbursement procedures (if applicable) and reporting requirements.

A common route for small nonprofits to receive government grants is to be a subcontractor or partner in a collaborative grant with other organizations. Each partner should sign a memo of understanding or subgrant agreement to ensure that there are transparent goals and division of labor between organizations. This is often a better option for small groups as generally one of the partners takes the administrative and financial responsibility for the program.

Other Organizations

Many of the strategies listed above (appeals, meetings, grants) are appropriate for fundraising from other organizations. Corporations, law firms, unions, religious organizations, and small businesses all support nonprofit organizations. As with other fundraising, personal relationships are crucial to successfully raising money. Staff and board members should reach out to key partners and get to know them. Learn what are the priorities and appropriate ways to solicit support from these organizations.

Events

Many nonprofits raise serious money from events. There are so many different kinds of events, from backyard cookouts to fancy galas. Events raise money and generate awareness about your organization. Events need not be fancy or complicated. The more you can keep costs down, the more money will be raised for your organization. Ask your vendors or area businesses to donate or underwrite goods and services for the event. Think about having a breakfast event instead of dinner or holding a cocktail hour instead of a full meal. Also consider staff time in preparing for special events. Events can be a huge staff time investment but can provide great tasks for board members or active supporters to organize for the organization.

Because events are not just about raising money, be sure to create goals that are not just money-focused, such as inviting potential donors or engaging the board in the planning process. Also include a strong follow-up plan after the event to further involve those donors.

Benefit events. Honor special people in your community and raise money for the organization. You can sell tickets or tables, have event sponsors, create a silent auction, or sell ad book space to encourage additional giving. Some corporations, unions, and law firms only give to events or buy ad space, so it can be a good way to get support from groups that don't normally fund your work. Make sure you have at least one honoree that will bring in different types of groups to support the event because they like the honoree.

Participate in an event with other organizations. Sometimes organizations can raise money without being responsible for all of the planning and logistics for the event. In Minneapolis/St. Paul, Air America Minnesota invited a local celebrity to tape a radio show live to raise money for community organizations. Board members of the Twin Cities Religion Labor Network had connections with the planners of this event and encouraged the radio station to make the organization a recipient of the funds raised by the event. All board members and staff had to do were to sell and buy the $25 tickets to help raise money for the organization. One hundred percent of the ticket sales went to benefit the Religion-Labor Network and another community organization.

Hold a house party. Board members or donors can hold a small event at their homes for their friends and family to hear more about the organization and support it financially. There is usually light food and drink, a brief presentation, and a request for support. House parties needn't be elaborate or expensive, and can be successful with as few as 15 to 20 guests. It is important that the invitation states that guests will be given the chance to support the organizations so that they will not be surprised by the solicitation.

Another approach to house parties is to not solicit at the event, but develop a plan for each attendee to meet with a board member to build a relationship. The individual may then contribute at a much higher level than what would have occurred when passing the hat at a house party.

Other grassroots events. Some organizations hold barbecue fundraisers, wine tastings, carnivals, races, walks, and much more. The most effective events seem to be ones that have a strong connection to the organization and its work. Think about what type of event would speak to your constituency and make plans around that.

In-Kind Support

Not all organizations will have the resources to give to your organization directly, but they may be able to provide important in-kind support. This could include free/cheap office space, copying services, or meeting rooms. Some corporations, high schools, and religious congregations also have lots of people who might volunteer.

Businesses, law firms, and corporations often provide goods and services to help nonprofits. Businesses can donate items for a silent auction or food for a fundraising event. Lawyers, accountants, and bookkeepers can all provide pro bono legal and financial services, saving the organization a large amount of money. All of these services have value for your organization, especially those that you would pay for if you didn't receive it for free. Review the finance section of this manual to see how to account for in-kind gifts.

Your fundraising sources should be diverse and continuously expanded. Don't stop fundraising in some areas because you got a large gift. Instead, think of that gift as an opportunity to expand your work and grow your fundraising even more!

Chapter 3: Thanking Your Donors

Thanking someone for a gift is as important as receiving it! Thanking your donors is an important part of raising money for your organization, and it's probably the most underutilized and forgotten part of the process.

A major donor at a nonprofit organization gave $500 a year but had to contact it at the end of every year to receive an acknowledgment letter for her taxes. After the third year of not receiving her letter, she stopped giving. It had nothing to do with the organization's good work nor her belief in the cause, but rather its poor administrative systems.

Another donor wanted to make a gift of stock to a nonprofit. It took the nonprofit more than three months to set up a brokerage account (it should take a week or so). Then, after the donor gave more than $10,000 worth of stock, she had to ask three times to get a letter acknowledging the gift. She will never give that organization a big gift again.

> Donors that give to your organization deserve to be thanked carefully and in a timely manner. When preparing to thank a donor, consider:

Who thanks? A formal thank-you letter should be sent promptly from the organization. In addition, an informal thank you can be sent from those members of your organization who have relationships with the donor, such as a staff person, a board member, or a volunteer.

When? Contact the donor as soon as possible. The general rule fundraisers use is to thank donors within 72 hours of receiving their gifts. A common refrain is to "thank before you bank," so don't wait to make a deposit to acknowledge the donor.

How? The more personal the contact, the better. In-person visits, phone calls, or handwritten notes are powerful ways to thank donors. If it's not possible to arrange such personal responses, the organization could print out form letters and add a personal note to each letter. Electronic acknowledgments should be sent right away for online gifts. Many software programs automatically send a response after the gift has been processed.

The content of your letter can be standardized, but if you can, make a personal reference in the letter. Try to mention a past phone call or meeting that you had with the donor. It's great to give updates on your work in a thank-you note that urges current donors to give again and again. For example, it's appropriate to tell donors that their contribution will help young people get jobs. Or that their gift will help provide educational materials to 300 workers employed in dangerous industries. Your donors will be proud that their dollars are being used in such concrete and important ways!

This is also a great way to engage board members, especially those members without much experience in person-to-person fundraising. Ask board members to make thank-you calls for donors above a certain dollar amount ($100 or more) just to thank them for their support.

Why? Thanking donors strengthens the relationship between your organization and donors, which could lead to future gifts. Timely thank you notes show your donors that the organization is well run. It also shows that your organization values all gifts from $10 to $10,000. All are received with gratitude.

A written acknowledgment is also required

for the donor to claim the gift as a donation for tax purposes if the gift is $250 or more. Finally, staff, board members, or volunteers get the opportunity to acknowledge others' generosity. They also have the opportunity to reconnect with friends or acquaintances in the process.

Effectively thanking your donors can be of tremendous benefit to your organization. With the help of staff, board members, and volunteers, thanking folks in a personal and timely way proves an effective method to build and strengthen your organization.

Legal Requirements.

It is very important to comply with legal requirements when your organization acknowledges a gift it has received. The laws on charitable giving occasionally change, so do some research to make sure gifts are acknowledged in accordance with current requirements.

Cash gifts/noncash gifts under $250. Your organization should acknowledge the gift to the donor but is not required by the IRS to give a written statement with any special language. However, because you plan to provide a thank-you note to the donor, it doesn't hurt to include a statement reinforcing the idea that no goods or services were provided in the donation.

Cash gifts/noncash gifts of $250 or more. For your donor to receive a tax deduction, your organization must acknowledge the gift in writing with a statement that no goods and services were provided in exchange for the donation. This can be put at the bottom of your thank-you letter or within the letter itself.

An example of such a statement is:

> "No goods or services were provided in exchange for your contribution. This gift is tax deductible to the extent allowed by law."

In all cases, the thank-you letter should include the name of your organization, your 501(c)(3) tax-exempt status, description of the gift received (amount if cash), and the date the gift was received. The letter should also include how the donor will be acknowledged in publications. Donors should be given the option to give anonymously.

For noncash gifts (like office furniture, computers, or other equipment), the fair market, or estimated value should be included in your thank-you letter. This value must be *given by the donor.* Ask the donor the value of their gift when she/he donated it to you.

If the noncash gift is valued at more than $5,000, then the donor needs to provide a written appraisal of the gift before receiving an acknowledgment letter from the organization.

More information on these gifts can be found in *Charitable Contributions, www.irs.gov/pub/irs-pdf/p526.pdf.*

There are special rules for certain donations. Rules for car donations can be found in *A Charity's Guide to Car Donations, www.irs.gov/pub/irs-pdf/p4302.pdf.* Other rules are created as patterns of giving change, so regularly read up on charitable giving laws and policies. The *Chronicle of Philanthropy*, listed in the bibliography of this section is a good resource to get current information on these laws. Your accountant or tax attorney should also know detailed information on gift acknowledgment.

Gifts from special events, raffles, and auctions. The deductibility of a gift is reduced when a donor attends an event because the donor gets something of value in return (dinner, music, entertainment).

Tax-exempt organizations that receive donations in which part of the contribution is a gift and part is in return for goods and services give the donor a receipt detailing how much of the contribution is a gift (deductible) and how much is in exchange for goods and services such as meals, entertainment, or books (nondeductible).

Example: Your organization decides to hold a fundraiser that includes a cocktail reception at a hotel. You sell tickets for this event at $100 a piece. You determine that the fair market value of your event is $30 per person, which is the cost for the hotel room rental, food, and live music. Every person who buys a ticket for $100 can deduct a maximum of $70 as a tax-deductible contribution. The donor will receive the following written statement as a part of the thank-you letter:

"Contributions over the value of this event ($30) are tax deductible."

Raffles and the cost of raffle tickets are not tax-deductible. Be sure not to put any language on your organization's tickets that refers to the tickets as donations.

More information is found in *Charitable Contributions Substantiation and Disclosure Requirements, www.irs.gov/pub/irs-pdf/p1771. pdf*. Raffles are also governed by state laws on gambling, so research the topic before moving forward.

Stock Gifts. Stock gifts are considered non-cash gifts and require slightly different acknowledgment.

The description of the gift should include the number of stocks, company name, and date that the organization received the gift. An example is:

> "Thank you so much for your gift of 25 shares of IBM stock, which were transferred to Interfaith Worker Justice on March 10, 2013."

Some nonprofits have a policy of selling stock on the date in which it is received and so know the value of the gift. Others provide a mean price of the stock on the date the stock was received and assign a contribution value that way, regardless of when the stock will actually be sold. An example is:

> "On the date your gift was received, based on a high of $210.74 and a low of $209.43, the mean price of the stock is $210.08. The value of your contribution is $5,252."

Good Administrative Systems for Thanking Folks

Small nonprofits often get behind in thanking their donors because their systems are disorganized. Good structures to develop include:

Regular bank deposits. As much as possible, deposit checks or credit card gifts *before* a thank you letter is done. There are occasions when the gifts bounce or are declined and it's more work to get a revised letter out to the donor. Regular bank deposits also makes sure financial reports are accurate and that money is not sitting too long in the office.

Clean data. A maintained database will make it easy to pull the data to run regular thank you letters. For gifts, good database fields are donors name, amount of gift, date gift given, and date gift deposited. Sometimes donors lose their letters and ask for copies, so you must be able to find their gifts and re-create thank you letters.

Easy mail merge. Create letter templates with standard mail merge fields that are the same as the database fields. This will enable you to export the data you need and easily insert it into a word processing program.

Save some letters. Because the letters are personal, keep files on the major donors. Consider creating folders (hard copy or online) for each person/organization that gives more than $500 total in a year and keep copies of correspondence related to that person or organization. These files will help with fundraising and any future staff that need historical information.

Change your thank you letter occasionally. Having a form letter is okay, but change it at least once a year to reflect the theme of your fundraising appeal or update language and stories related to your work.

Although legal information and systems are crucial, the more meaningful reason to acknowledge donors is to build a relationship and engage them in your work. The personal approach will certainly help with the relationship, but also remind the donor of why the gift is important and how his or her support will help create a better society.

Chapter 4: Staying on Track

Good fundraising requires good tracking systems. It's a long term process and needs systems to build upon over time. Consider the following tools to stay on track with raising money.

Database. The database chapter (Section 3, Chapter 1 on page 74) of this handbook explains in much more detail why a database is important and how to get started. In the fundraising context, a good database allows you to communicate with your donors through mail, phone, or e-mail. It should have a record of gifts made by each individual or organization that make it easy to see the patterns of giving. You can also record how the person got into the database (staff, board, Website, Facebook), which can help with doing fundraising outreach.

Your database should also be able to run simple financial reports such as LYBUNT (Last Year but Not This Year) or reports of donors listed by total gift. This can be helpful in seeing which donors need a nudge to give again, or if there are donors that are giving several times a year or regularly that should receive special attention.

Foundation Tracking Sheet. Once you start making contact with foundations and writing grants, it is very important to keep track of grant deadlines and the amount of support you raise for the projects in your organization. The chart below is just one way to keep track of foundation deadlines. The important thing is to have a tracking system that works. You would hate to miss out on getting a grant because you missed the deadline! Foundations also ask for this type of information in grant applications, so keeping good records can make grants even easier to finish.

FOUNDATION TRACKING SHEET

DEADLINE	SOURCE	$$ in 14	$$ in 13	$$ in 12	PENDING	TO ASK	CONTACT	NOTES
Core Support								
1-Aug-05	My Community Foundation		$20,000	declined		$30,000	Jane Smith	Invite her to our event
Youth Leadership Program								

Fundraising Calendar. Grants need to be tracked, but there's usually a million things going on that all need to be coordinated into some kind of messy harmony. A fundraising calendar can be incredibly useful to map out dates for the strategies outlined in the fund-raising plan.

Microsoft Word has a calendar template (Click File, then New from Template) that is nice because it provides a visual picture of the deadlines. It can also be printed and taped to a wall or shared with others pretty easily.

Files. If files are organized, you know where things are. Files can be hard copy or electronic (or both), but must be kept complete. If only electronic, be sure to have a scanner so that correspondence that comes in the mail can be scanned.

Files that should be maintained include:

- *Foundation files.* These files should be organized in alphabetical order, with the new information on the top. Include any letters or important e-mails received from the foundation and copies of anything submitted to the foundation like grant applications, reports, letters, and financial documents. Also include notes of phone calls or meetings with program officers.

- *Major donor files.* These files should be organized in alphabetical order, with the new information on the top. Include any important correspondence between the donor and organization, meeting notes, letters, or thank you notes.

  Do not organize individual donors by putting their information in the appeal/campaign folder that they gave to! One new nonprofit director wanted to reach out to past major donors to introduce herself and start to build relationships. She couldn't find their past giving unless she knew which direct mail campaign they

had donated to! It was impossible to see a donor's total gift history or learn much about donors with files organized this way.

- *Other organization files.* Most other files should be organized in alphabetical order (government grants, corporate gifts, matching grant programs). If there is any business, religious groups, or bank that has given you a significant donation (like $500 or more), it's worth starting a file.

- *Fundraising solicitation samples.* Keep hard copies of direct mail appeals and mailings you might repeat in future years with letter, form, and envelope organized by date.

- *Event samples.* Keep hard copies of program books, ad books, sponsor lists, sponsor solicitations, and anything else that might be valuable for future fundraising and organizational history organized by date.

- *Leadership file.* Both staff and board should have easy access to who has served on the Board of Directors, during what period of time, and who served in leadership roles. This information is helpful if and when an organization decides to start a planned gift program. It might also be helpful if the organization is ever called to provide a tribute to an individual in the past who contributed to the organization's leadership.

Maintain all electronic copies of files on the organization's computer server or the computer that holds the organizational history and knowledge. The electronic files can be organized just as above, with a few additions:

- *Organize the foundation files in two ways.* Whoever writes the grants should organize the files in two ways. One set should be alphabetically by foundation name and by year. That way it's easy to see what applications were developed and during which time period. The files should have all the information that was completed and sent to the foundation, including program description, financial reports, and any attachments.

The other way is to create folders per program area that receives/should receive grants and copy the application materials for that program into its own folder. For example, if your organization receives grant money from a corporation, a foundation, and a religious order to support your program to develop youth leadership, all of those applications should be copied from their alphabetical folders and put into a Youth Leadership folder together.

The reason for this is that all the language related to that program can be found in one place for future applications. Grant writers, once enough language is developed, should be able to copy and paste certain sections for multiple applications. It's difficult to do that if you don't remember which foundation you applied for each project.

- *Develop folders for common documents used again and again.* You need a whole slew of documents for any type of grant or even for charitable trusts or employer matching gifts. Keep all of your organizational documents in one place and organize them by year if they change. This could include:

  - *Financial.* Audit, 990 Form, Current and previous year's budget, previous year profit/loss, Balance Sheet
  - *Fundraising.* List of current funders, foundation tracking sheet, fundraising plan
  - *Legal.* 501(c)(3) letter or fiscal sponsor letter
  - *Internal.* List of Board of Directors, with names, affiliations, addresses, staff list, and organizational chart

Often you don't create a document until you need it, like a form that graphs the racial and gender diversity of your board and staff. But it's possible you will need it again in the future, so put a copy of it electronically in a common document folder. That way you won't have to remember which foundation application required it six months from now. Interfaith Worker Justice has a common folder that everyone uses called "LOOK FOR IT HERE." When in doubt, that is where staff look for the commonly shared documents.

- *Keep your thank you note templates.* You don't need to keep a copy of every thank you note sent, but do keep the electronic file of your thank you notes by year. Your thank you letter should be changed at least once a year, and it's helpful to be able to see what was done in the past.

Taking the time to develop good files and systems is an effective use of time. It is also more efficient when you can always find what you are looking for in the future!

Chapter 5: Fundraising Resources for Small Nonprofits

There are more fundraising trainings, webinars, books, and magazines than on any other administrative topic, and many are really good.

Books

These authors have very practical, accessible styles to their materials. They are also great trainers, so try to see them in person if possible!

Ahern, Tom. *How to Write Fundraising Materials that Raise More Money,* 2007. Also has a good blog at *www.aherncomm*.com.

Flanagan, Joan. *Successful Fundraising: A Complete Handbook for Volunteers and Professionals,* 2002.

Klein, Kim. *Fundraising for Social Change,* 2001, and *Reliable Fundraising in Unreliable Times,* 2009.

Robinson, Andy. *Grass Roots Grants. An Activist's Guide to Grantseeking,* 2004.

Warwick, Mal. *How to Write Successful Fundraising Appeals,* 2013.

Websites

Guidestar, www.guidestar.com. A national database for nonprofit organizations. This is an excellent resource and probably one of the most popular sites for grant makers and grant seekers. Includes a free service that allows nonprofits to list their missions and program information online. For grant seekers, most foundations are listed along with recent 990 forms.

The Foundation Center, www.fdncenter.org. A good foundation search engine to find contact information, Websites, and most recent 990 forms. It also includes information on

training programs, the current state of philanthropy, and other related topics. You can register for free electronic newsletters.

Federal Register, www.gpoaccess.gov/fr/index. html. The all-purpose daily journal that contains, among other things, announcements of federal grant competitions, funding priorities, and proposed changes in grant regulations. You can search the *Federal Register* by keywords (e.g., "disabilities AND grants") and/or by a range of dates.

Catalog of Federal Domestic Assistance, www. cfda.gov. A catalog that contains detailed descriptions, contact information, and funding levels for the more than 1,200 federal grant programs. The online version is searchable by keyword, agency, type of assistance, and eligible applicants.

Training Resources

Grassroots Institute for Fundraising Training, www.grassrootsfundraising.org. This organization focuses training and resources for social justice fundraisers, especially those in community-based, grassroots nonprofits.

State Associations of Non-profit Organizations, www.councilofnonprofits.org/salocator. This Website provides a list of state-based associations, most of which provide materials, trainings, and library locations for nonprofit organizations.

Network for Good, www.networkforgood.org. This organization is best known for its credit card processing services. It also has free fundraising resources and webinars.

Community Foundations and Other Funders. Many community foundations offer capacity-building and training opportunities to their grantees. The help comes in all forms (workshops, printed resources, consultants, networking groups) and is generally free or low cost.

Magazines/Periodicals

Blue Avocado, www.blueavocado.org. This online magazine is easy and fun to read, and covers all types of back-office topics, including fundraising. The subscription is free and automatically sent in an e-mail.

The Chronicle of Philanthropy, www.philanthropy.com. This is a good resource for current philanthropy trends, successful fundraising strategies, and interesting editorial pages. It also has a national foundation list with grants awarded and upcoming deadlines.

The Grassroots Fundraising Journal, www.grassrootsfundraising.org. This journal gives you the best nuts-and-bolts advice for fundraisers working with membership organizations. Every issue has good ideas you can apply immediately.

Capacity-Building Grants

Sometimes there are opportunities to obtain grants to solve capacity-building issues. Community foundations advertise capacity-building grants to streamline administrative issues, help build a major donor program, or get a new database.

You could also approach a current funder and ask for a discretionary grant to fix a pressing problem. If your organization already has a grant, you might think about a fundraising or back-office issue that directly connects with the program for which you receive funding.

Grants are often most helpful when sup-

porting staff time, buying equipment, or underwriting training. Consultants are often suggested by foundations, but be thoughtful on what makes sense for your organization. The best lessons are often learned through experience.

> **Fundraising** is all about building relationships and trust.
>
> If you don't ask, people won't give.
>
> Follow instructions!
>
> Plan, Plan, Plan
>
> Thank, Thank, Thank
>
> Have fun!

Conclusion

Nonprofit leaders demonstrate values every day. They work hard, stand up for what is right, and do the best they can to work for an equitable and just world. This manual is one way to deepen those values on how nonprofit organizations are run.

No one organization is run perfectly. So consider the information here as an aspiration of what your organization might plan to do over time. Leaders should affirm the good practices already in place and continue building from what you have.

Every new year brings with it a new opportunity for planning, growth, and change. This applies not only to program work but operational and financial practices as well. Prioritizing internal procedures will result in a stronger organization that does an even better job of changing the world.